P9-CDL-168

Please remember that this is a library book,
and that it belongs only temporarily to each
person who uses it. Be considerate. Do
not write in this, or any, library book.

WITHDRAWN

WITHDRAWN

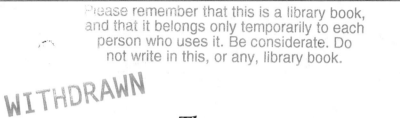

The
Reading/Writing
Teacher's
Companion

INVESTIGATE
NONFICTION

The Reading/Writing Teacher's Companion

B170047

The Reading/Writing Teacher's Companion

INVESTIGATE NONFICTION

Donald H. Graves

HEINEMANN
Portsmouth, NH

IRWIN PUBLISHING
Toronto, Canada

Heinemann Educational Books, Inc.
70 Court Street   Portsmouth, NH 03801
Offices and agents throughout the world

Published simultaneously in Canada by
Irwin Publishing
1800 Steeles Avenue West   Concord, Ontario, Canada L4K 2P3

© 1989 by Donald H. Graves. All rights reserved. No part of this book may be reproduced in any form or by electronic or mechanical means, including information storage and retrieval systems, without permission in writing from the publisher, except by a reviewer, who may quote brief passages in a review.

Every effort has been made to contact the children and their parents for permission to reprint borrowed material. We regret any oversights that may have occurred and would be happy to rectify them in future printings of this work.

Library of Congress Cataloging-in-Publication Data

Graves, Donald H.
  Investigate nonfiction.

  (The Reading/writing teacher's companion)
  Bibliography: p.
  Includes index.
  1. English language—Composition and exercises—Study and teaching.   2. Language arts (Elementary)
I. Title. II. Series.
LB1576.G7276 1989   372.6'23   88-26811
ISBN 0-435-08486-0

Canadian Cataloguing in Publication Data

Graves, Donald H.
  Investigate nonfiction

(The Reading/writing teacher's companion)
ISBN 0-7725-1716-9

1. Report writing—Study and teaching (Elementary).   2. English language—Composition and exercises—Study and teaching (Elementary).   3. Language arts (Elementary).
I. Title.   II. Series: Graves, Donald H. The reading/writing teacher's companion.

LB1576.G74   1989   372.4'23   C89-093196-8

Designed by Wladislaw Finne.
Printed in the United States of America.
10 9 8 7 6 5 4 3 2 1

VCgift

**To
*The Children of
Central America***

---

*May their future
be rich with health,
learning, and
opportunity.*

contents

about this series

Reading and writing are both composing processes. History shows they have been kept apart. This series, The Reading/Writing Teacher's Companion, brings them together. With these books as a guide, you can explore the richness of reading and writing for yourself and for children. You can improve your own listening, experiment with learning, and recognize children's potential in reading and writing. Five books will make up the series:

- *Investigate Nonfiction.*
- *Experiment with Fiction.*
- *Discover Your Own Literacy.*
- *Build a Literate Classroom.*
- *Explore Poetry.*

The approach to teaching and learning is basically the same in all five books, although each stands alone in its focus. All five emphasize a learning style that immediately engages you in trying literacy for yourself, then the children. So much of learning is, and ought to be, experimental. A series of "Actions," experiments for personal growth and discovery in the classroom, are highlighted in the text to help you develop the kind of literate classroom you want. The Actions are ordered in such a way that you will gradually become aware of children's growing independence in some aspect of literacy. In all five books I'll be trying the experiments right along with you.

The five books stress learning within a literate community. Reading and writing are social acts in which children and teachers together share the books and authors they enjoy and their own composing in the various genres. Make no mistake, individuals are important, but good classrooms have always stressed group as well as individual responsibility.

The books also stress the importance of your own learning within a community. When you try the Actions and enter into new experiments with your teaching, you ought to consider reading and learning with colleagues in order to maximize your own efforts to grow as a professional.

acknowl-edgments

Help for this book on reading and writing nonfiction has come from many quarters. Observations of our six preschool grandchildren responding to the queries and expectations of their parents have served to give me a new appreciation for language, forms, and genres.

At the recommendation of Nancie Atwell I made several visits to Donna Maxim's third-grade classroom in Boothbay Regional Elementary School in Boothbay Harbor, Maine. I am indebted to Donna and her children for showing me how an entire curriculum can be taught through children's literature. Her understanding of children, curriculum, and literature demonstrated how the best of writing can help children learn to think and appreciate the world around them.

Jane Hansen read chapters as fast as I completed them. She supplied several good examples of young children's early process thinking. Jane has spent the last two years observing the operation of the library and librarian at the Stratham Memorial School in Stratham, New Hampshire, as part of our three-year study of evaluation. Her knowledge of children's literature in content area work has been invaluable to this book.

Once again, Nancie Atwell has given running commentary via phone and letters about the conception of this book. She has a sound, no-nonsense notion of what helps teachers and children. Mary Ellen Giacobbe has drawn on her own personal library of children's books to recommend good read-aloud books in nonfiction.

Don Murray has helped. He has read the text and kept me in touch with my own voice as he has done for my last fifteen years in New Hampshire.

Teachers at the Stratham Memorial School have begun to extend process work across the curriculum. The type of literature read by children now moves from fiction to nonfiction, extending the base of genre in their extensive reading.

Encouragement for continuing this work in nonfiction came from students in the Advanced Reading/Writing Institute at the

1988 University of New Hampshire summer program. They read, used, and critiqued early drafts of this book. Last March Julie Powell and Linda Henke from West Des Moines, Iowa, responded to still earlier drafts.

For three years Philippa Stratton, Editor-in-Chief at Heinemann Educational Books, has guided The Reading/Writing Teacher's Companion series, which began as one book and now has become five. Patience and persistence are her hallmarks. This book and this series would not have been realized without her leadership.

Donna Bouvier, Manager of Editing and Production at Heinemann, has sensed the spirit and intent of this book and then focused on the details that must be in line with an author's purpose. I am grateful to her for her expertise and the spirit with which she has brought this book to final copy.

My wife, Betty, though appearing last in this list of acknowledgments, must stand at the forefront of important help with the book. Her work with a medical team in Honduras and her continual focus on children's needs in Central America brought home to me the need for a nonfiction text that helps children in the United States to be more precise in understanding the points of view of people around them. It was Betty's work that made me more sensitive to the needs of children in Central America and to the importance of their future. This book is dedicated to them.

roots of nonfiction—
discourse

Recently, I was sitting in a friend's living room drinking a cup of coffee. We had made an appointment to plan for a conference. Her young daughter, about eighteen months old, was playing in the background. In the midst of our conversation, the little girl brought me a stuffed animal and plopped it into my lap. Hardly missing a beat in conversation with her mother I said, "Oh, thank you, Marcy." Within a few minutes Marcy returned with another stuffed animal and deposited it in my lap next to the first one. Again I thanked her, this time naming the animal: "Oh, thank you for the little lamb." In the next fifteen minutes Marcy brought thirteen more stuffed animals to me until my lap and the couch were overflowing.

I doubt that Marcy was making a deliberate attempt to impress me with the number of stuffed animals she possessed. What she did was to act out one of the many ways of transacting information. She took objects from her room, objects of the same class, the animals, and on presenting them to me received a response to the transaction, a thank you and a different name for each. Next time she might name the objects herself as she deposits them.

Children accumulate "heaps" of information when parents read to them about animals in the barnyard or show them pictures of the many kinds of whales in a picture book. Soon children are touching the pictures with a finger, delighting in the naming of all classes of things as they are presented on the page. Information is inherent in multidimensional objects that can be held, in a picture in a book, or in an imperfectly spoken word.

Language exists to aid in transactions. A child requests something a parent has by extending a hand. "Muk, muk, muk," he repeats. The child wants milk. The child receives milk. Transaction completed. In later years, this same child begins to realize the power of print. He comes to his mother just before bedtime and gives her a note. The note reads, "can I wsh TV." The mother is impressed and allows him to watch just a little more

1

television. The child, sensing that the mother values literate events, has consciously used print instead of asking her, "Mommy, may I stay up to watch one more TV show?" The child receives an immediate reaction to the note. He doesn't have to wait. The whole transaction could have been handled through speaking, but the child chooses to write, realizing in this instance that print has more power.

On another occasion, a girl's mother arranges for her to go next door when she gets home from school, to stay with the neighbors while her mother goes to the doctor. "Take the key and go in to change your clothes and then write me a note to say you went next door so I will know that's where you've gone," her mother instructs her. This time print is used to communicate information in another place and time. This is a different transaction from what has occurred before. Soon, Laura's mother is writing notes to Laura when she cannot be present, putting notes in her lunch for school or under her pillow at special times, or letting Laura know she has noticed certain things Laura has done. In this way she demonstrates again and again the power of print to give a sense of a personal presence.

The need to communicate gives rise to various forms and structures, and the forms developed in the home continue to be needed when the child goes to school. As the demand for information and expression becomes more sophisticated, the structures become more formalized and require more convention. Let's take a look at some of the forms young children need to use to communicate before they even enter school.

WHAT HAPPENED? Two-year-old Anne falls and scrapes her knee in the driveway while chasing after her dog, Brownie. She runs to her mother, who is trying to fix the back door. Through her tears she cries, "Brownie . . . knee [*pointing to it*] . . . hurts." Her mother tries to reconstruct the event, puzzling over Brownie's involvement. In this instance, Anne chooses essential words to try to recount the event. She must rely on context to help her, although she is not aware she is using this strategy. Her mother tries to reconstruct the event in order to understand Brownie's place in the incident. Although she doesn't succeed, Anne has demonstrated the beginning of personal narrative, an attempt to recount an event to someone.

The ability to compose a story about "what happened" is one of the fundamental units of human thought and knowledge. Recounting in order with an interpretation of events is the underpinning of all human thought. Without it there would be no history, geology, chemistry, biology, or physics, to name but a few disciplines that rely on an orderly recounting of events.

Anne is beginning a lifelong journey with language, which starts with the naming of her universe and then moves on to recount events that connect what she can name. Long before Anne tried to tell what happened when she fell while chasing her dog, her mother read her stories and recounted events, real and fictional. Anne is familiar with the "and then" process and may even intone the "and then" markers in her speech, just as her mother did in her reading or storytelling. Anne is also learning that the marks on the page, along with the illustrations, represent a consistent rendering of events. Read again, they say the same thing each time. Her mother holds the book with Anne and the same sounds and words come from her mouth each time she reads the marks on the page. Not only is the story the same, but the same words always follow each other in the reading (recounting) of what is on the page.

When Anne fell down, the words she used to tell about it gave a passionate account of what happened. The words were not a mechanical statement; rather, her cries and "hurts" were the beginning of the interpretation of meaning. She possessed data and reported her ordering of the facts in a tone that might persuade her mother to comfort her.

INTERPRETATION   In one sense, all narrative accounts are interpretations of an event. They are ordered so that the listener's attention is held, so that the listener might be persuaded and impressed by the person telling the tale. In some instances, the teller editorializes about the event and thus moves into beginning essay or exposition. Note the way this child interprets as she tells what happened (interpretive text elements are in italics):

CHILD: I went over to the playground *but my mommy said I shouldn't cross that street*. We played on the swings. *The swings were dangerous because the other children went so high.*

When parents tell stories and comment on the meaning of those stories, they use language to talk about language as well as about the events themselves. This is important background for children, who need to understand the function of exposition. If there are different sources of data or contrasting stories about the same event, so much the better.

When Anne enters school she will have many opportunities to recount events. When the children share information with her, she will want to tell them about her new baby brother, her dog, or where she has been on the weekend. If she has been observing the newly hatched chicks in her classroom, when it comes time to tell about her observations she will need to use narrative. If the other children ask the meaning of what she has seen, she will need to expound on her data using information from her observations to support her conclusions.

INVENTION   As I mentioned earlier, all narrative is invention. That is, it is impossible to give a completely precise accounting of an event because of our sensory limitations, biases, and desires. Audiences also affect what we choose in a story. Some children, however, regularly narrate fiction when recounting real events, enjoying the feel of an outcome they wish had happened. In some cases, unless the listener was present, there is no way to tell if the story is fact or fiction.

SHOWING OR DISPLAYING

Anne stands at the top of a mound of dirt pushed together by a bulldozer. "Dad, Dad, lookit," she shouts. Anne wants to show she has climbed to a high place . . . all by herself. She also likes the feeling of being almost as high as her father is tall. Anne scribbles and rushes to show her paper to her parents. She buttons two buttons by herself or drinks all her milk. Again, she wishes to show her accomplishment, the fact that she is doing "big" things.

When Anne is able to complete something that involves a process, like setting the table, clearing some dishes, helping to weed in the garden, or finding a book that has been lost, it is a good time for one of her parents to confirm the process that has accomplished the task. Her parents act as "historians" by asking for an account and a demonstration of something that worked. Anne then tells and shows how she went through the task from beginning to end. Many times Anne simply won't know what she has done, yet by asking the question she creates the schema "How did I do it? It is good to know." She is discovering that there is a process to most everything you do —and that it is useful to know it and to tell the story to your mother or father.

When Anne is in school, her teachers will continue the same types of information transactions, asking her to indicate how she accomplished a task, especially when the task went well. "You managed to finish cleaning up, Anne. Good job. How did you do it? Tell me from the beginning if you can remember." The ability to recount a process is the forerunner of one of the most difficult kinds of writing: directions. Recounting a process is the foundation of observation and recording in sciences such as chemistry, physics, and biology.

PLANNING

Anne looks out the window, sees some children playing in the snow, and says, "I want to go outside, Mommy." Anne has expressed a plan. She opens the closet door knowing that her snowsuit is inside and that putting it on is a necessary prelude to going outside. Anne's wish to go outside was triggered by the image of children at play. Yet she is able to express a wish about the future and to begin to execute a process that will lead to play. Anne acts for the future, basing her actions on a personal history that includes a process, probably language mediation by her mother, who has talked her through getting ready, and a sense that she will be permitted to express plans that can be carried out.

As Anne gets older, she will be able to rehearse plans on the basis of her reading of the context, any relevant process information, and her ability to hypothesize. (The child who wrote the note "can I wsh TV" to his mother made a request, but it was also a plan for future action, a proposal.) Later, Anne will write directions to order the details of a process for someone else. This means that she will have to have a strong sense of the process as well as the ability to represent the event to herself and, at the same time, to decenter and read the directions from another point of view. This is one of the most difficult composing tasks, but one that has its origin in the early years of using language to affect the future.

DUAL POINTS OF VIEW   Throughout her early years Anne will encounter contrary points of view. Although she asks, Anne might not be permitted to go outside. Her mother cites her reasons: "Anne, I know you want to go outside, but you can't. You are just getting over having an ear infection, so today you can play with your dolls, your blocks, or perhaps something else you'd rather do." Anne's mother uses a structure Anne has heard many times: acknowledgment of her feelings, reasons why she cannot go outside, and an alternative plan. The structure can be useful as a literate form for the rest of Anne's life—acknowledgment of another point of view, the rational facts in opposition, and a proposal for alternative action—for persuasive writing, argumentation, and report writing. If children are unfamiliar with this type of structure before they come to school or with any of the other structures mentioned here, then the school will have to supply them.

Dual points of view are also illustrated in good children's literature. I especially recall Mairi Hedderwick's book, *Katie Morag and the Two Grandmothers*, in which Katie sees two entirely different personalities interact with each other. There are countless illustrations of dual points of view in parent/child relationships. Robert Munsch's book, *I've Got to Go*, the story of a child who has to go to the bathroom at the most inopportune times, produces a good-humored profile of child/parent differences.

SUMMARY Most of the forms that children use in their acquisition of language and in their daily transactions at home have their counterparts in rhetorical structures in writing. Literate, oral communication that attempts to deal with complex transactions requires reason and negotiation. Some of the types of transaction have been reviewed here. In summary, they are:

- *What happened.* Children need to be able to give recountings of what has happened to them or of events they wish to share with others.
- *Interpretation.* Shared events need interpretation. "This is how it happened and why I think it happened that way."
- *Invention.* Children (and adults) will invent data to go with their accounts and interpretations.
- *Show or display.* Children wish to display their skills and share the process of how they do things.
- *Plan.* Children need to be able to use language to structure a future, project a request, hypothesize, or give directions to others.
- *Dual points of view.* Children encounter different points of view throughout the day. They need to understand the logic behind other points of view and at the same time have their own points of view confirmed. Children

encounter these structures and narratives that deal with other points of view in the literature that is read to them.

Whether these oral forms are developed in the family or the neighborhood, or whether the child encounters them in print, they are very important for the child's entrance into school and ultimate success in reading and writing. Make no mistake, reading and writing are different from oral discourse, but the basic forms of oral communication are important underpinnings for future thought. What is good for the home is good for the school. Whether or not the child has come from a home that uses these types of transactions, they must be either continued or introduced, since they are basic to the types of literacy demanded for further thinking in school. In the next chapter you will see how these various forms continue to be used within the classroom.

2

*transitions from oral forms
to reading and writing*

Schools need to continue the effective language structures learned at home that produce good communication. If these structures are undeveloped, then it is even more important that teachers use them in the classroom. They are not contained in language arts textbooks, nor can they be developed through workbook exercises. They develop because the teacher attends to the child's message, frames it, extends it, and, above all, helps the child to become a member of a community of persons who help each other to convey hundreds of messages the teacher knows nothing about.

The purpose of this chapter is to explore the many occasions during the school day that allow children to continue their language development. I will consider the same structures that were demonstrated in Chapter 1. Although oral to written transitions occur throughout a person's life, the focus of this chapter will be the early school years, kindergarten through grade two.

Throughout this book you will encounter headings entitled *Actions*. Actions, as their name implies, are teaching approaches to try—yourself or with children—that put us "in motion" with experiments in learning. Where possible, try the Actions with a colleague so that you can share the experiences and experiments from your own classroom. Or you may not want to try the same Actions together, but you will be able to share your victories and discuss some of the problems you've encountered. A great deal of theory is embedded in the chapters that follow, but any theory is meaningless unless you try it out for yourself. Furthermore, you will be formulating your own theories from observation of children and practice with them. The Actions are your opportunity to take charge of your own learning and teaching.

Although this book is about investigating nonfiction, it does not mean that children should write only nonfiction or that it should be the only approach to writing and reading. Rather, I have highlighted the elements of nonfiction so that you can see what is involved when you work with certain children who are sustaining work in this genre. Children should be writing in many genres: fiction and poetry, as well as the several varieties of nonfiction.

ACTION: LOOK FOR OPPORTUNITIES DURING THE SCHOOL DAY WHEN CHILDREN CAN TELL STORIES ABOUT "WHAT HAPPENED."

When children burst through the door in the morning, their faces are marked with what has happened to them. Their untold stories encompass the full range of experience, from sadness and pain to joy and discovery. Their stories are often contained in a single line:

- "Look, I've got new shoes."
- "My dog just had puppies."
- "The cops stopped a car at the corner."
- "My mommy is sick."
- "I forgot my lunch."

These story offerings usually include a principal agent and an action, which serve as cues for a teacher to help children expand the telling. "Oh, tell me about getting your new shoes," or, "Oh, start from the beginning and tell us about the cops and the car at the corner."

If children, especially in kindergarten and first grade, know that they can tell their stories early in the day, rehearsal for some may begin before they arrive, thus creating a more complete telling when they actually share their story. In my work with children, I lean much more to storytelling—short narrative accounts—than the more classic "show and tell," in which children bring in objects. Sometimes objects do enhance a story for children, but the object should function as a prop to a story rather than as a "look what I've got." Many teachers begin the day with sharing, or they have children go to work immediately in interest centers and then pull them together forty minutes or so after the beginning of the day, because they prefer to move throughout the classroom listening to individual children.

ACTION: HELP CHILDREN TO TELL PROCESS STORIES ABOUT HOW THEY
WORK AND LEARN.

When children complete a task or when they are in the middle
of their work, ask them how they have done their work to this
point:

TEACHER: John, I noticed that you just cut this out very
   nicely. How did you go about it?
JOHN: Uh, I don't know. I just did it.
TEACHER: Well, just tell me from the beginning. Pick up your
   scissors and make believe you started and just tell me
   while you do it.

At first, children are unprepared for questions that ask them
how they have done things. For young children especially, the
past is a vague, amorphous zone of existence: "yesterday" refers to all the events of their lives before "today." This is particularly true in process stories. The task of doing the "new"
is often so demanding that process steps are obliterated. But
the process question can activate the structure and, in time,
help children to begin to ask themselves: "How did I do that?"

During sharing time ask children if they have any stories
about how they accomplished their tasks. Or point out areas
where you suspect there are unusual process stories to tell. "I
see that Robbie kept the same story going to a second page. I
bet Robbie has an interesting story to tell about how he learned
to do that."

When children become adept at telling process stories, and
other children find them useful, they begin to state plans: "Know
how I'm going to figure this out?" "Know what I'm going to
do next?" The ability to recount is strongly connected with the
ability to plan, and the ability to plan is often ultimately connected with the ability to write directions and produce logical
arguments. Sometimes teachers will write down a process statement by a child and post it with the child's name and date to
emphasize the fact that children are problem solvers and can

supply problem-solving language. Here are some examples of process statement situations:

- This is how I figured this word out.
- This is how I learned to read this page/this book.
- This is how we cleaned the area up so fast.
- This is how we saved some paper.
- This is how we learned to share this book.
- This is how I sounded this out so I could write it.

ACTION: LOOK AT CHILDREN'S DRAWINGS AS A SOURCE OF INFORMATION FOR TEACHING.

Usually children's first attempts to show narrative on paper are in the form of drawings. Before they begin to convey the passing of time in their drawings, their compositions are quite static. Figures (through their relative size and their juxtaposition on the page) are used to connote meaning rather than shown actually "doing" something. The "doing" is usually supplied through oral interpretation: "This is a bird and he wants some food" refers to a drawing of a bird in a tree.

Long before they write words on paper, young children are able to show events through their drawings. Observing how children use time and space and figures on the page will help teachers understand how they are depicting events. The drawing, the "hieroglyph," is an intermediary between oral and written discourse. At the same time, it should not be seen as something a child will outgrow. Pictorial representation continues to be a valuable tool for externalizing thought into adulthood—as such professionals as physicians, engineers, and writers will attest.

Florence Damon, kindergarten teacher at the Mast Way school in Lee, New Hampshire, demonstrated just how well children could show process stories, even though at the time only a few could read and write. At Halloween, Florence carved a jack-o'-lantern out of a pumpkin with her children. As she did so, she showed in a series of drawings the sequence she followed from first incision to final product. Later, she asked the children to show something they had done or observed in a four-step sequence. The drawings and writings in Figures 2–1, 2–2, and 2–3 show that these children, some of whom knew how to begin writing, others not, could handle this exercise, a foundational one for future development of thought.

ACTION: BEGIN TO WORK WITH SOURCES OF INFORMATION.

Although some children may begin to write in personal narrative, many do not. A careful examination of children's early composing reveals lists and "heaps" of information like Greg's early composing: "Tr ar tnks hnd granads flm thrws an mns" (There are tanks, hand grenades, flame throwers, and mines). Greg wanted to show his acquaintance with many kinds of weapons. Children enjoy lists and attribute booklets in the form of "all about" stories related to areas of personal interest. These may be the easiest and most elementary forms of information for them. Susan Sowers (1985) noticed this phenomenon when she wrote about children's nonnarrative writing during the Atkinson study. Observe children in kindergarten and first grade who merely label their pictures with a one-word invented spelling. One might say the label is the precursor to the list, and the list is an important base to specifics contained in narrative writing. On the other hand, some children use simple directives or signs, such as "Kep Of" (Keep off).

The written narrative is the extension of the personal story but comes later in the scheme of things. Children need to tell stories about themselves in order to anchor their own experience. The kind of recall involved in personal narrative is one of the easiest. Children remember what happened to them. The girl who drew the process of a bird starting to fly did a recall of what she thought was involved. The reporting was immediate, and the response of the other children was immediate. For children in kindergarten or grade one, when a piece has

FIGURE 2–1   CROSSING THE STREET

FIGURE 2–2   OPENING THE WINDOW

FIGURE 2–3   HOW A BIRD FLIES

been completed, it is finished. There usually isn't that much interest in returning to the operation.

In spite of children's high interest in the present, the process of working with a cumulative past is one of the foundation stones for writing nonfiction. Effective nonfiction writers work from an information base—a base of information that accumulates. The teacher assists in long- and short-term data-gathering expeditions. When Florence Damon drew pictures to represent the various stages of cutting out the jack-o'-lantern, she reenacted the task. She brought the past into the present by reviewing the process; she used short-term data gathering.

FURTHER EXAMPLES OF SHORT-TERM DATA GATHERING The class gathers data because the data will be needed again. Charts, graphs, pictures, material read in books, interviews, numerical counts, all are useful because both teacher and children will need them again. In short-term data gathering, they will usually need to use the information within several days.

Children should begin to be involved in data gathering through the daily information tasks that every classroom requires. Here are some typical examples:

- Daily attendance.
- Lunch counts: milk and hot lunch.
- Lunch money: children from kindergarten to grade two can be apprenticed to an upper-grade child to conduct this daily operation.
- Book circulation from classroom or central library.
- Regularly shared activities such as reading or writing.

Any one of these tasks can be charted if instruction is given on how to keep graphs. As soon as children can count, they should become involved in this type of data gathering. I find it helpful to pair children up and have the stronger member of the team teach the second member. In all of the above examples, the teacher can introduce each process in three to five days (less or more depending on class ability). The children can do it along with her to see how it is done. Then a child who seems to understand the process best can team up with another child who is trying it for the first time on his or her own. The first team may need two weeks of practice to carry the process out effectively, but before the year is out, children will have taken the responsibility to see that everyone can do it.

FIRST INTERVIEWS The interview is one of the cornerstones of information gathering throughout a child's career as a learner. People possess information and have opinions, they have read and done lots of things that give them knowledge they ought to share with others. An easy way for children to begin to learn about interviewing is through simple polling of classmates. A team of two children take a clipboard and poll classmates on information the rest of the class might want. The teacher can choose several items to show children the potential for polling and conduct a sample poll herself, moving quickly around the circle of children. Here are some polling examples:

- Which do you prefer: breakfast, lunch, or dinner?
- Which do you prefer: morning or afternoon recess?
- Which of these TV programs do you prefer? (The children have decided which three they would like to learn about. Up to five programs may be listed if the teacher thinks the children can handle the extra record keeping.)
- Which of these is your favorite game? Team?

The team of two children move around the room asking the interview question of the day. It is often difficult for the children, especially when they are inexperienced, to remember which classmates they've questioned. To solve this problem, one of the interview team members can carry a sheet with everyone's initials, and the child interviewed can find his or her initials and circle them. When all the initials on the sheet are circled, the children know the interview process has been completed. The interview sheet looks like the one in Figure 2–4.

FIGURE 2–4   AN INTERVIEW SHEET

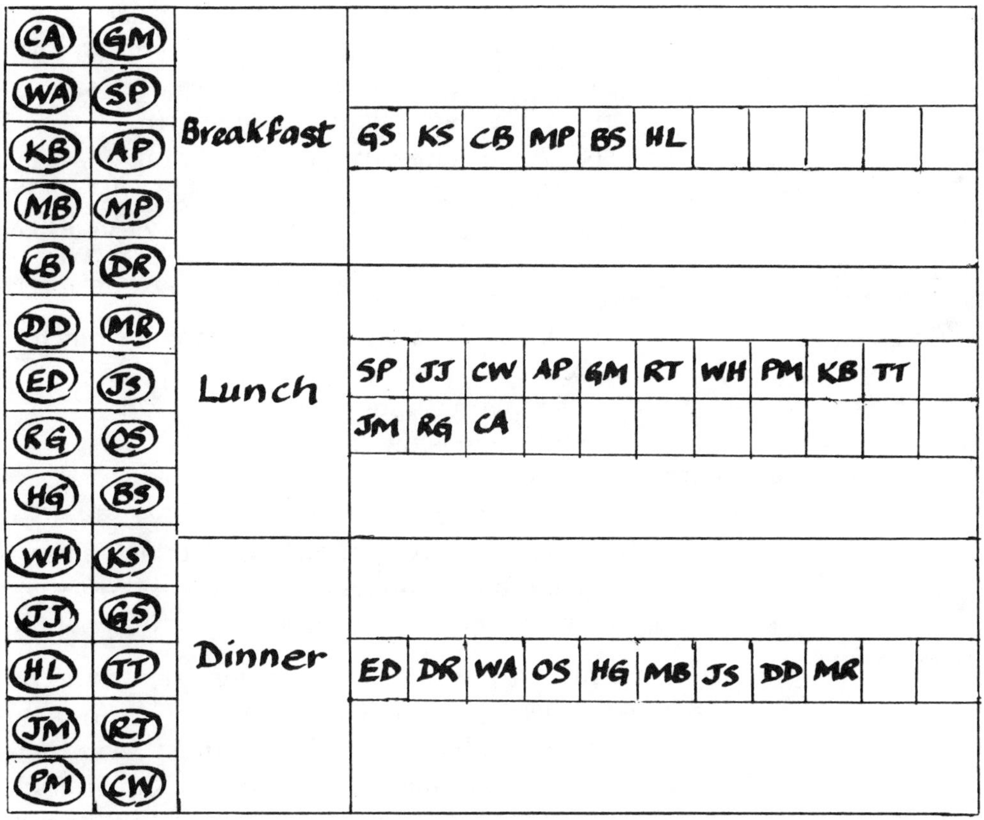

CA	GM													
WA	SP	Breakfast		GS	KS	CB	MP	BS	HL					
KB	AP													
MB	MP													
CB	DR													
DD	MR													
ED	JS	Lunch		SP	JJ	CW	AP	GM	RT	WH	PM	KB	TT	
RG	OS			JM	RG	CA								
HG	BS													
WH	KS													
JJ	GS													
HL	TT	Dinner		ED	DR	WA	OS	HG	MB	JS	DD	MR		
JM	RT													
PM	CW													

USING THE INTERVIEW
DATA

The interview sheet needs to be large enough for children to see. If the children are gathered together in close quarters—on the rug or on the floor—they will be able to see the bar graph that evolves opposite the polling. A discussion can follow:

TEACHER: We have the sheet here that tells what you decided about what you preferred [*points to each graph component*]—breakfast, lunch, or supper. Alice and Betty have asked each of you which one of these you liked most. Now, what do you see here [*pointing to the chart*]?

CHILD: I see where Alice put the mark for mine.

TEACHER: Yes, that's the way Alice and Betty did it. They put a mark, just one mark for what each of you liked. What else?

CHILD: Most like lunch.

TEACHER: Count them. Let's see how many for lunch.

CHILD: There are thirteen.

CHILD: And supper has nine.

TEACHER: Which one is the lowest?

CHILD: Breakfast.

TEACHER: How many? Six. Good, now I've got to do something so that I won't forget all that you've told me. I want to write these number stories down. [*Writes on an easel, chalkboard, overhead, or experience chart paper.*]

There are many other types of questions that could be asked and other observations that could be made about this very simple graph. Graphs can be demonstrated even more concretely by having the children stand in rows according to their decision (the lunch row, breakfast row, etc.), thus helping them to realize that each person stands for a number. Data are people; numbers stand for people.

INTERPRETATION

You can also ask the children to state why they made their choices, encouraging them to consider their reasons. After the "breakfast people" have made their statements the teacher could ask, "Well, after hearing all these reasons, is there one that seems to be pretty nearly the same for everyone?" The data are generalized and, at the same time, abstracted for decision making. You can then ask the next type of question: "Well, if people like lunch the most and only a few like breakfast, what does this mean?" Data, and the interpretation of data, are the foundation blocks of future essay writing. Practices like these can begin early in a child's school career.

Interpretation also accompanies discussion about books that have been read aloud to the class. Effective interpretation, interpretation that helps children to prepare for more effective nonfiction writing, begins with the facts of the situation, the "what," and then expands into explanation (as shown in italics):

TEACHER: You say the boy wanted the dog very badly. Would you say some more about that?

CHILD: Yes, he had been feeding the dog for a long time, and he didn't tell his mother.

TEACHER: Why?

CHILD: *His brother was allergic to dogs, and he didn't want the dog to go away but he didn't want to lose him either.*

In this instance, the teacher elicits more data so that the child will draw some inferences about the meaning of what the boy has done. This is the same structure the children used in their interviewing project: first the data, then the interpretation. The above interchange could have been about a story the child had read, an episode that occurred at home, or something that had happened to a friend.

An important caution must be mentioned here. Often it is too easy to fall into the trap of gathering "what" data and always following with a round of interpretation. Teaching is a craft, and sensitive teachers know when interest in "what" is present or potentially activitated through their assistance with a question. Analysis paralysis is the hallmark of too many American classrooms.

DUAL POINTS OF VIEW Greg was an incensed first grader. He discovered that papers were being pushed under the door of his classroom from the second grade on the other side of the door. He approached his teacher, Mary Ellen Giacobbe, with a request to "go in there and tell them to cut it out."

"No, Greg, you can't, but I suggest you write a note to help them understand what you think about the matter." Greg wrote a short, cryptic note: "Stop pushing papers under the door."

"Do you think that will work, Greg? Why do you think that will make them stop?" Greg agreed that maybe an order wouldn't help. He went back to work, this time pointing out some of the problems caused in his classroom by the papers coming under the door.

Wherever there are disagreements, dual points of view, whether they occur in the books children read, in controversies between children, or in variations of opinion on any subject under the sun, the potential for argument is present. Disagreements are excellent places to discover the power of discourse forms. A frequent issue in schools is "big kids picking on the little kids on the playground." As the children poured into one classroom with anger written on their faces after a frustrating recess, the teacher pulled them over to sit down on the rug. Quietly she took a large sheet of paper, put it on the easel, and drew a line down the middle. "All right, what happened?" The children were used to that phase of writing. They poured out a list with vitriol. "The big kids take our balls; they push us around; they want the whole playground; they yell at us and say bad names."

After hearing the children out and listing what the "big kids" had done on the left side of the paper, the teacher then asked: "Now pretend you are fifth graders. Let's try to list their reasons on this side. Make them up. See if you can think like a fifth grader. I'll write a list here on the right side of the paper." Although the children may respond with many short narratives about "what happened," the list here is intended primarily to give an abstraction through a listing of words.

As the year progresses, children should be able to write one-sentence opinions and list one or two facts to back up their cases. You can provide a writing opportunity after there has been a good discussion of the subject. The children write on smaller slips of paper, which can then be tacked on a bulletin board. Several children may even wish to classify the responses, categorize the reasons given for the problem, or even offer a solution. Children should have many experiences like these in working with data classification and summary.

OBSERVATION Direct observation is an important source of information. Our lives are filled with hundreds of processes occurring simultaneously at any given moment within a few feet of us. As I sit in my study, I see chickadees, redpolls, and finches (both gold and purple) at the bird feeders outside my window. The smoke from my neighbor's chimney goes straight up, indicating that there is not much wind today. The sky is a special blue, meaning high pressure will be around for a while. Wood is burning in my stove; the hissing I hear is from a wet piece of wood that didn't get enough seasoning in the sun. Mozart's Piano Concerto no. 20 is playing on a compact disc, and I wonder at the principles that extract sound from the shiny disc. Some flowers lean in a vase, their florets and leaves looking tired, since they are past peak and in the process of decay. The sun is rising in the sky and the intense light patterns are traveling from left to right across the rug. The temperature is 22 degrees outside, and the snow crystals are starting to thin on the surface. There is a wet sheen to the ice as the sun strikes it, the first melting showing in the sheen.

ACTION: LIST THE PROCESSES UNFOLDING WITHIN TWENTY FEET OF YOU.

The list I quickly jotted down above is very short. I left out how I was changing at the very moment I wrote the words down. Change is all around us, and we need to be aware of it. The world is changing, and literate activity is one way of coming to understand that world. Understanding change, the hundreds of processes around us, is what literacy is all about. Drawing, recording, and reflecting on the sequences of activities help us to see differently. The present tense of our lives becomes a more beautiful, perceptible event. There will be discrepancies in what we see that cause us to scratch our heads and ask further questions, which demand still more observation.

If children are to see the world differently, we as teachers must also see it differently. After you make your list of observations, choose one to describe in greater detail. I am going to take ten minutes to write about my neighbor's dog, which has just been let out of the house this cold March morning. I will write rapidly, changing nothing; what follows is my first draft:

I've never really observed my neighbor's dog. She is old; that's about all I carry in my mind's eye, but now I watch her as she has just been let out first thing in the morning. She walks. She doesn't run or even trot. Head down, she walks with feet splayed a little like an old bear will head for the dump. Her tail is not raised above her back; rather, it is drawn slightly in and down between her legs as if to keep her bottom warm. It is icy footing with yesterday's melt an icy glaze. Now the dog, a brown, black and white mongrel of collie background, border collie size, sniffs intently at one spot; she circles, sniffing still more intently, never raising her head. But she moves on from that spot waddling another twenty laborious steps until she stops to check the day. Her head bobs up and down in erect posture, the sun warming her face as she must wonder the meaning of odors that drift her way. But the sniff is no cause for action; bored, she waddles her way toward the street never changing the pace of her morning walk.

I chose the dog because of the ease of observation. Her actions (if she *is* a she) are deliberate and easy to record. Anything that moves has a process. Anything alive is filled with simultaneous processes. From this day forth I will never see my neighbor's dog the same way again. My observation and my writing have raised more questions: Is the dog female or male? Does it have arthritis? How old is it? How far did the dog roam? How long does the dog stay out? What is the dog's name? This dog has lived next door for the last three years, and I am shocked by how little I know about it. It is also an indication of how little I must know my neighbor that I know so little about that dog.

The intent of this kind of exercise is to help you be aware, as a professional, of the number of processes around you. You can list them, but to choose one to write about is to place yourself in the position of learning still more. In the classroom, I make a list on the chalkboard of all the things the children see happening. This usually means listing anything that is moving—inside or outside of the room, although I try to limit the list to what is near us.

SHORT-TERM OBSERVATION

Like the process of recording through interviews, the kinds of observation discussed in the following sections bridge the gap between oral and written communication. You begin with short-term observation, that is, data recorded in the course of one day. The actual amount of time for observing and recording should be limited to a maximum of ten to twenty minutes. Here are some examples:

- Count how many autos cross a particular point in front of the school.
- Record how many birds you can see flying in the space of ten minutes (use an egg timer).
- Watch one bird and tell how the bird flies.
- Watch one gerbil or hamster and record what it does.

When children observe, they will need to learn how to record their data by making marks or using a tape recorder. In the case of the gerbil, they will need to develop a language of key words to record behavior. (You might observe the hamster first and list words for the children to use, assuring them that the animal may do something you haven't recorded a word for yet.)

When the data have been gathered, they can be shared with the class in "report" form—a table or a graph. It is also important to place the children's findings in a folder to be kept handy and used from day to day. For example, a series of observations done each day by teams of two children can be bound together as accumulated data for daily reference. This approach combines both short- and longer-term observation. By reviewing past data and speculating about what the data may show in the future, the children are preparing to understand both the purposes of data gathering and the longer-term data-gathering process.

LONGER-TERM OBSERVATION

When children are used to short-term observation and have experienced the power of information, some longer-term observational steps can be introduced. The challenge throughout this transitional period is to use the data to communicate—with parents, other classes, or visitors to the classroom. It is also important for teachers to refer to the data. "What did the gerbils do yesterday?" "How many cars passed in front of the school yesterday?" Data are collected in order to be used. That is the power of printed records.

Children are used to the eradication of the past. Their life is "now" oriented. When they have completed a drawing, children hardly look back to contemplate the final act. When children play with blocks or trucks at home, each step replaces the previous step. They rarely return to previous operations. In speaking, the children cannot return to previous words unless they have used a tape recorder. Even then, it is nearly incomprehensible to them that the words coming from the recorder were recorded at another time. The use of data—print recorded at another time—will also be new and, like prior recordings, nearly lost in the moment. Asking questions or discussing past data will fall in the same category. The look on a child's face communicates puzzlement: "Why would anyone want to return to what we've done? Let's get on with something new."

Longer-term observations can last for indefinite periods. I need to introduce a note of caution here about my own advice. Longer-term data gathering need not necessarily wait for successful work with short-term data gathering. Children can maintain an off-again–on-again interest as they gradually come to understand the meaning of data recording.

Somewhere in the school yard or near it, mark off a piece of land with stakes. Allow about a ten-by-twelve-foot piece. (Sometimes marking the piece off with string or stone markers is helpful.) The purpose of this longer-term data-gathering project is to note the many kinds of change that occur on this one small piece of land over a year. The land does not have to be in the country. As long as there is something growing, even if it is only weeds, the project can be successful, since where there is life there will be change. It should be possible for everyone to stand around the outside of the plot to see what may be on the land. The first step is to see *what* is there. Here are some things to look for:

- *What is growing?* Grasses, leaves of any kind; look for anything with green. You may have some evergreen types that won't change, but usually the flat broad-leaf type of foliage will change over the course of the year. With this kind of foliage it will be possible to do a series on the fading of foliage in the fall and the coming of foliage in the spring. For this (if there is enough vegetation), I take one leaf each day, iron it between pieces of waxed paper, and put it on a sequence chart. This will show how the leaves go from full green to yellow or red (and then ultimately fall). If you can choose a plot that has a tree on it, so much the better, since many changes will occur in the tree in the course of the year. The tree will also support and encourage many kinds of life beneath it. You may even be able to attach a hanging bird feeder to the tree in order to observe the many kinds of birds in your area.

- *What is moving?* Look under rocks and leaves. Get next to the bark or even leave some biodegradable material like bread, candy, or anything sweet. The material will soon be covered with insects. Look for ants, crickets, and spiders. It will be helpful to carry a magnifying glass with you to look at things in greater detail.
- *What are the effects of weather?* What happens when there are changes from hot to cold, or there is snow or rain? You may be able to keep track of snow with a small stake marked off by inches to record depth.

These are only a few of the possibilities for observation. Naturally, there are regional differences in foliage, bird, tree, and insect life, and you will want to call your local Audubon Society for assistance. If you are near a college or university, a call to the public relations department (to reach the most appropriate department) could help. Many books, written for both teachers and children, can assist you in your "land" venture. Some books are for reading aloud to children, to help them understand what may be happening on their plot of land. These include books like the following:

- Ruth Heller, *The Reason for a Flower* (New York: Grosset and Dunlap, 1986).
- Ruth Heller, *Plants That Never Bloom* (New York: Grosset and Dunlap, 1984).
- Ruth Heller, *How to Hide a Whippoorwill and Other Birds* (New York: Grosset and Dunlap, 1986).
- Peter Parnall, *Apple Tree* (New York: Macmillan, 1987).

The above books were chosen because of their rich use of language and their scientific accuracy.

There are many other ways to encourage children in longer-term data gathering. Go to your local florist or supermarket and pick up some narcissus bulbs. Narcissus bulbs are ideal for measuring growth because they shoot up so rapidly, from bulb to stalk to blossom in three weeks' time. Place them in crushed rock, water, and they will grow with minimal care. Children can use graphs to record growth, numbers of buds, etc.

Weather is another natural element to record over time. Records can be kept on precipitation (snow or rain), barometric pressure, cloud formations, and the length of shadows at various times of the year.

FINAL REFLECTION ON TRANSITIONS

In this chapter, I have aimed to involve you and the children together in beginning the transition from an oral culture to a more graphic, written culture, in which children learn with greater precision the power of print. The world is constantly changing: the height and weight of the children in the classroom, weather systems, the uses of energy, the whole universe inside and outside the classroom—all reflect that change. Keeping records on the changing world through drawings, marking down frequency, telling number stories about change, and even hypothesizing about what may change next are all important foundation stones for the treatment of information in exposition and argument, and for all the transactions needed to understand what print can do.

Children interview, record, and write because they will need the information again—for themselves and for the many audiences who will find the data useful. Children collect data about the weather, from interviews, from the "land," and about class opinions to get a sense of the change in the world and, therefore, the changes occurring within themselves. Data are collected not just to have heaps of information, but to provide opportunities to rethink and interpret, to hypothesize and predict what may yet come, and to observe the trends and patterns information may reveal. You and the children together can develop the power to observe, to note change, and to delight in reporting the many "fast-breaking" stories around you.

put nonfiction to work

As they grow older, children will need to write more extensive nonfiction pieces because issues will arise in the classroom that require their use. Some children will be able to start this type of nonfiction as early as second grade. Several points of view emerge as children discuss their interpretation of a text, a classroom issue, or a political question. In their earlier years, they may have only talked about such matters. Now they discuss their positions and the positions of others and write about them. Point of view takes on more complex dimensions as children express themselves more formally than in kindergarten or grades one and two.

In keeping with this developing use of nonfiction writing in the intermediate grades (3–6), you write letters to individual children or even respond in writing to their thesis statements and supporting evidence. The children are expected to write back, answering questions and asking more questions in return. Writing and reading are used much more "for export" than in the earlier grades. Children write letters of invitation to experts to invite them to visit the class. They write letters of concern to the main office about school issues. Occasionally, they may write letters to town officials or other community members. During the upper-elementary years, children ought to see the impact of their literacy beyond their own classroom. I mention letters here because the letter is the foundation for the essay.

An examination of the writing folders of children in the intermediate grades reveals a broader range of genres, especially in nonfiction, which now includes the essay, the letter, directions, formal and informal argument, satire, and humor. These uses of writing have expanded because the teacher has responded to a particular occasion within the classroom community and introduced the forms through mini-lesson workshops. Because they are introduced within the context of classroom issues and events outside the classroom and the school, the forms become relevant; to a large degree, children see how these forms of writing will serve their own needs. At the same time, the teacher has also encouraged children to experiment with a number of nonfiction forms. The children's reading diet has also changed. When they initially began to shift from basal readers to other kinds of reading, their first interest was fiction. Now they have expanded into biography, historical fiction, information books, and nonfiction books in areas of special interest. The purpose of this chapter is to show how nonfiction forms can be appropriately discovered in classroom situations.

LETTERS Children can begin writing letters before they go to school. When I notice that my son has just fed the dog, I can write, "Thank you for feeding the dog, Bill." Although it might have been easier to speak the words, there is something about writing down the actual text that adds emphasis and authority. By taking a little more time, I make the act of feeding the dog more permanent.

When parents or teachers write notes and letters to children, they sometimes receive notes and letters in return. The examples I've used here are letters that get an immediate response; the child or parent presents the note and receives a response. Parents can increase the space-time dimension by placing a note under their child's pillow when they have gone out for the evening or in their child's lunch bag.

Letters are actually meant to communicate with someone in another place at a future time. I think the thing that bothered me most about my early letter-writing experiences was the "have to" letter, or thank-you notes: thanking people for birthday or Christmas gifts was nearly unbearable. Thank-you letters are important, but they are a poor introduction to letter writing. When the Christmas present is two weeks "old," the notion of thanking grandmother for something I can barely remember is tough going if it is the exclusive diet for letter writing. Furthermore, grandmother probably won't write a return letter. In short, the letter originally intended to be a communication really isn't.

As much as possible, I'd like children's first experiences with letter writing to be a series of responses; that is, letters go back and forth regularly enough for the contents of one letter to be the basis for the next. Teachers can do this in the classroom when they write to children and request a written response: "Write back." One of the main points to make about a letter, especially in the classroom, is that you (the teacher) don't have time to have as many individual conversations as you'd like. Furthermore, you can have much more substantive conversation via the written word. Of course, this approach works best if the subject is both substantive and personal. Here is an example:

Sarah, I see that you have been interested in books by Beverly Cleary. In fact, you've read three now and I was wondering which way you were headed next. As you have already seen, Beverly Cleary is quite an author. Which of these books do you like best so far? Well, that's two questions, but I couldn't help asking them. You are doing good work and I was wondering where you were headed next. Write back.

In her book *In the Middle* (1987), Nancie Atwell shows better than any writer I know how to maintain a dialogue with a student. And dialogue is important. Conversation, written conversation, becomes successively layered as it moves toward more in-depth thinking. Nancie, on occasion, didn't hesitate to say, "Write back; I want to know."

Most letters are written to one person. Think of it: one person, not a committee, a Board of Education, or a faculty of teachers. As such, letters ought to be as direct as a conversation, avoiding delays in sharing or requesting information and at the same time providing space for the person who will respond to the letter.

ACTION: EXPERIMENT WITH VARIOUS TYPES OF LETTERS.

First, try experiments with letters yourself. Letters are certainly governed by the persons to whom we write. As in most conversations the speaker adjusts to the person hearing the message. Just as in speaking, however, sometimes the speaker doesn't know the person to whom she is speaking. For example, here is a letter I wrote to my senator last week after a harrowing experience. I don't know the senator personally, but as I wrote I tried to consider how he might react to my situation. Here is the actual rough draft as I composed on my computer:

Dear Senator Rudman,

I am writing to you on my computer from Air Canada Flight 803, leaving Logan International Airport for Toronto. At approximately 11:37 a.m. while in full throttle for takeoff, the pilot jammed on his brakes, burning rubber, but narrowly missing an incoming flight crossing overhead at 90 degrees to land on another runway. At the last possible second the pilot was signaled from the control tower to abort takeoff. I fly several times each week and I am becoming more aware than ever of reported "near misses".

Something is wrong. Either there aren't enough air controllers, they are overworked, inefficient or whatever. I would like to know if this incident has been reported to the FAA. I want to know at least if the system for reporting such incidents is working.

For cross reference purposes the pilot was Captain D—— of Air Canada. I suspect that you must use Logan Airport yourself and share my concerns. I would appreciate a check by your office to FAA to see if this episode has been reported. Thank you for your assistance.*

I began the letter by reconstructing the event—an apparent near-miss on takeoff. I wanted the senator to have my version

---

* Senator Rudman replied to my letter and forwarded it to the FAA. The FAA said that no near-miss had been reported.

of the details and to realize that, as a citizen, I was upset by what had happened. As a citizen I also want to know if such matters are reported. Furthermore, since I assume that the senator uses the same airport, I thought he would want to be informed as well. If I were to write the letter again, I'd begin differently, stating my sense of urgency more clearly:

I was just involved in a near-air collision while taking off from Logan International Airport. I want to know if the system for reporting such incidents to the FAA is working. Here is what happened:

Air Canada Flight 803 at 11:37 A.M. on March 9 had to abort takeoff because another flight was landing at right angles to ours but in the same airspace as ours. The control tower called for the pilots to abort both flights . . .

I think the second letter shows more distance from the event. The first version was written a week earlier, approximately ten minutes after the event occurred. The first letter is characterized by a "Wow, look what happened!" tone, the second, by a "we must look very carefully at these matters" point of view. I suspect that there is a place for both kinds of letters, the impassioned "just happened" type and the more carefully formulated letter. The point is to write.

Think of an episode you'd like to call to someone's attention and write rapidly, trying to convey the immediacy of the event. Here are some letter occasions to consider:

• Call the attention of your local government to something you appreciate (or dislike) in the town where you live.
• Let your congressman know what you see, think, and feel about a national issue. You aren't seeking to make the congressman do something as much as to say what you think.

- Write a letter to a tradesman stating your appreciation for or concern about a job that was done in your home or on your automobile.
- Write a letter to a physician (minister, priest, rabbi) stating your appreciation for or concern about help and service.

Letters are marvelous opportunities to discover what you think about many matters in your life. All writing is an opportunity to find out what you think. Listen to your words as you write them down and let them reflect details, thoughts, and images.

Most letters, however, are written to someone we know. Telephone calls have taken the place of much letter writing. Letter mail, or mail identified as first class, has decreased significantly over the last twenty years. When I cross the road to my RFD box and open the flap, I find a crust of junk mail. Occasionally there is a handwritten or obviously personal letter in the barrage. Looking through mail these days is like weeding June peas after a two-week layoff—lots of weeds for very little gain. I enter the house with a fistful of mail, pull over my bright yellow wastebasket, sit in an easy chair, and weed the mail. When I'm done I've thrown away ten pieces for every piece I've kept. Occasionally, one of the envelopes I keep contains a personal letter. Even more rare is a letter that isn't asking me to do something or buy something. The friendly, chatty letter, the letter filled with sharing, joy in living, or an acknowledgment that the person recognizes me as a distinct human being is far down the yellow brick road. Most of these letters have been supplanted by the telephone call.

But I'll swap a friendly letter that is a true conversation for a phone call any day. It gives me a chance to experience the conversation many times over. I can read, reread, and exchange imaginary, extended conversations with the person. In short, the letter allows me to create something between us that is far richer than a telephone conversation. Make no mistake, my phone bill would appear to prove me wrong: invariably I call just after writing a letter, or write a letter just after a phone conversation, just to keep the dialogue going.

ACTION: EXPERIMENT WITH SEVERAL TEN-MINUTE LETTERS.

I will write several short, ten-minute letters now in order to experiment with two approaches to a conversation on paper. The first is a much more informal letter than the one I wrote to Senator Rudman. As I write—in this case to Bill Strong, a friend in Ogden, Utah—I imagine the face of the person I am writing to. This letter will simply be an attempt to show the person to himself.

Dear Bill,

It was such a pleasant surprise to see you and Carol at the hotel a week ago. I knew I was in your territory but I figured you would be two hours or so north by the time I arrived in Salt Lake City. There is something special about seeing a friendly face in a crowd of several hundred people whom I don't know. For some reason when I speak to a large group like that, if there are at least three to four people in an audience I know, then the talk becomes like a conversation with them. You may have noticed that I glanced over your way a number of times during the talk. That was especially true when we had the small group session in the hotel lobby.

As usual we just start talking as if our conversation had been interrupted by only a few minutes. The last time I saw you was in Durham, or was it at NCTE in Los Angeles? Anyway, I remember Durham, though we didn't get the time we wanted for a good long conversation. It was especially nice to meet Carol last summer. One thing that struck me, Bill, was the number of persons you introduced me to who had published their writing. These weren't casual articles either. In two instances you introduced me to people who had published novels. The Utah Writing Project is on the march!

Thank you for taking me to the airport. There is something special again about leaving a place with friends. It's the same way on arrival. The last memory of a place as a place of friendship marks the location differently. I wonder why that is the case. I remember talking about noticing the full moon the night before. You and Carol had observed it too. Yes, special. I wonder where we will see each other again. Please give my best to Carol and thanks for the chance to see you again at the Conference.

This type of letter seeks to focus on the person I'm writing to. I just want Bill to know how much the occasion meant to me and that it was good to get in touch again, nothing more.

The second ten-minute letter will be more like a dialogue in which the conversation goes back and forth between me and the person I am addressing, Lola Mapes, a teacher in West Des Moines, Iowa.

Dear Lola,

This letter has been burning in my head for about a week now. I can think of two reasons. First, we didn't have a chance to talk after the demonstration. Secondly, I was so impressed by your children, I have to say a few words about them. There are some things I wish you'd say about your class. Perhaps you could take a moment to write about them.

When I walked out of your classroom last Tuesday morning my mind was racing. Talk about an impromptu workshop. The children were amazing. We didn't know each other but the way they constructed that piece of fiction about the two parents arguing was impressive. I think there were only two to three instances in which I can recall a need to challenge inconsistencies in what they were composing together. That kind of fiction workshop requires them to listen very carefully to how the story has been constructed in order to make plausible suggestions for the next part. Lola, the quality of their work was no accident. I told Linda Henke that that was the best fiction workshop I'd ever been involved in.

What I want to know is your perception of what went on. They are your children. What have you been doing that made it possible for them to do so well? What did you learn about your children from the workshop? What implications do you see for working with your children's fiction? As I read this over there are too many questions. Perhaps you could choose one or two and say what you think. Thanks again for allowing me into your classroom. Let's keep in touch.

The teacher and I both witnessed the workshop event. I want her to know what I can remember, so I share what I saw. But I also want her to write back, if she can, to report her impression of what went on. Since the workshop was an unscheduled event in the midst of a very busy day, we didn't have a chance to chat. This letter balances my personal reaction with my attempt to include the recipient.

Now write your own letter.

ACTION: WRITE LETTERS WITH THE CHILDREN.

The difficult part about writing letters is the timing. When I write letters to people, it is because the occasion calls for it. Children too deserve real opportunities to write, and I particularly want to be sensitive to those occasions in the ongoing life of the class when writing letters will enlarge the children's understanding of what letters can do.

As I talk about letter writing in a workshop with children, I demonstrate on the overhead projector. We choose someone we all know to write to. Depending on the age of the children, I will determine how familiar the person is to whom the letter will be addressed. Younger children will write to more "immediate" people—the principal, the librarian, the local policeman at the corner, or a clerk in a local grocery store. Ideally, I'd like to have someone who may reply with a letter or possibly come in to the classroom to respond orally. The following is an example of how one class and I composed a letter together in a short workshop. (I am using the overhead projector, experience chart paper, or the chalkboard.)

DON: Who are some people we know to write a letter to? This is going to be the kind of letter where we know the person pretty well. We all see the person at least two or three times a week.

CHILD: Mr. Brooks, the janitor.

DON: Yes. [*Puts name on board.*]

CHILD: Mrs. Donadio in the cafeteria. She likes us.

DON: Yes. [*Puts name on board.*]

CHILD: Mr. Wells from gym.

DON: Yes. [*Puts name on board.*]

CHILD: Mrs. Streeter.

DON: The principal, yes. [*Puts name up.*] Okay, that's quite a few names. Let's stop here and think of what you'd like to know from any of these people, or what you'd like to tell them.

CHILD: I wish we'd go back to playing kickball in gym. Let's write to Mr. Wells.

DON: Okay, we have a reason here. Any others?

CHILD: Mrs. Streeter—I wish she'd do something about the big kids taking over our part of the playground.

The class then makes a decision about which person to write to, considering what they wish to say and the person to whom they will address the letter. This shapes the strategy in the next part of the workshop—establishing what the children wish to say in terms of their sense of the person to whom they are writing.

DON: You have decided to write to Mr. Wells. What do you want to say?

CHILD: We wish we could go back to kickball.

DON: Why?

CHILD: It was a lot of fun.

DON: Tell me more about that.

CHILD: We could pick teams and stuff; there was more action in it.

DON: Well, what's the problem now?

CHILD: We don't like this dancing.

DON: Oh?

CHILD: It's so slow.

CHILD: The boys have to be with the girls.

DON: All right, I hear some of these reasons and I've written them here on the board, but now I'm going to switch to something else. You may find it hard, but because we are going to write him a letter we need to think a little about Mr. Wells. What's he like?

CHILD: He's big.

DON: He certainly is. [*Writes on board.*]

CHILD: He's funny.

DON: Like how? Tell me about a time.

CHILD: Oh sometimes when we have teams he'll give us funny names like, the toads, or . . .

CHILD: Or skunks.

DON: I get a little of the picture. I'm going to stop here and show how letters get put together a little like a conversation. I'm going to take what we've put down here and use it in this letter. [*The written text follows.*]

Dear Mr. Wells,

You are very big and you make us laugh. You did when we played games and you called us toads and skunks.

You write just like when you talk to somebody. The difference when you write, though, is that they aren't there, so you "make" them just like in fiction. Part of making them is maybe telling what they look like, what they've done or who they are.

Of course, sometimes they don't know you, or if they do, they need to be reminded. Let's stand over where Mr. Wells is. This may be hard, but what do you suppose he sees when he looks at you? Look at yourselves through his eyes.

CHILD: The kids are noisy. They don't make good lines.

CHILD: They like to laugh and like jokes.

CHILD: Sometimes they are late for gym and they don't like dancing.

DON: Stop right there. Let's take that and use it. You see if I get it right.

We are Ms. Janney's second-grade class. We are usually pretty noisy. We like to laugh and sometimes we are late for gym.

How does that sound?

Now for the part about what you want to tell him. We have that up here. I'll write here and see what you think.

We miss kickball. We don't like the dancing. There isn't much action in it. It's so slow and the boys have to be with the girls.

Now, we've got one last part. This may be the most difficult part of all. Why do you suppose Mr. Wells has dancing as part of gym? [*Long silence.*]

This is hard. Think some more.

CHILD: He has to do it because the school makes him.

DON: Maybe. Look, because this is so hard, perhaps we could ask him in the letter to come and tell us.

CHILD: Good idea.

We don't know why we have dancing. Maybe the school makes you. Will you come and tell us why we have dancing?

REFLECTION: LETTERS AND AUDIENCE

When writers write they "represent" their audience. Inexperienced writers need to be especially conscious of the "who" to whom they are writing, while experienced writers know how to build in a sense of audience because they are more aware of them at an unconscious level. As they write, they respond to the necessary, unspoken questions of the reader, engaging in a dialogue they may not be conscious of. This is what Flower and Hayes (1981) call "reader-based prose."

In most writing, the audience is covert; when readers read, they recognize themselves in the common questions and ambiguities considered by the writer. In contrast, the friendly letter in most cases is much more overt in the way it represents both the reader and the writer. The writer signals the reader that both are present in the text. This is what was going on in the exercise about the gym teacher, Mr. Wells. I took them through their concern about an issue to a representation of Mr. Wells and a representation of themselves, a simple matter of turn taking: "This is who you are; this is who we are; let's talk about an issue." In short, "Who are you, who am I, who are we together?" Writing and reading should result in the transformation of persons through a representation of each in text. Nowhere is this kind of transformation more true than in the directness of a letter, the exchange at one specific moment of a dialogue on paper. Letters should be one of the most fundamental, joyful laboratories for developing a rich understanding of what point of view is all about.

ACTION: HAVE CHILDREN EXPERIMENT WITH A LETTER ON A SINGLE ISSUE TO SOMEONE OUTSIDE THE SCHOOL.

The next experiment with letter writing focuses on writing someone in the local community or at the state or national level about an issue that concerns the children. The issue may come from something that has happened in town, a national news item shared during morning news, or even a question about endangered species or the local environment that has arisen during discussion in science class.

Teachers who are sensitive to occasions are constantly looking for "live" issues to use for demonstration during mini-lessons. We are eager to show children what reading and writing can do as we help them to understand and explore their world. In the early years, the issues are more immediate. They may range from disagreements in the classroom or within the school to the reporting of good things to other classrooms. As professionals, we are always seeking ways to expand the time-space dimensions of the children's world at every age, but especially in the older years. This means we look for opportunities for children to gather facts through reading and interviewing; we look for individuals outside the classroom and school with whom they can communicate.

The letter I wrote to Senator Rudman provides an example of how children can move out from immediate situations. Since I don't know Senator Rudman personally, my language was slightly formal, as if I were meeting him in person for the first time. Look for a similar occasion in the morning newspaper or the evening news, and when you sense an issue of more universal concern, show the children how to deal with it through writing. More often than not, if the issue is controversial enough there should be differences of opinion among the children, reflecting the pluralism in political belief within the community.

As I write this morning (March 1988), President Reagan has ordered 3,500 paratroopers into Honduras because of the reported incursion of Sandinistas across the border from Nicaragua. If I were working with a classroom of children this morning, I would see what the children knew about it and sample their feelings. Our dialogue might go like this:

TEACHER: Did anyone catch the news this morning? What did you hear?
CHILD: The president is sending troops.
TEACHER: To where and why? Tell me anything you can remember.

At this point the children might go on to list all they could remember. Because of the differences in political persuasion among the families represented by the children, two very different points of view would emerge. The two points of view would reflect different accounts of the same event and different beliefs about the necessity or lack of necessity for the president's action. The differences might be listed in two separate columns on the board:

GOVERNMENT VIEW

The Sandinistas invaded part of Honduras and chased the Contras. They are doing this because they want to defeat the Contras before the peace meeting starts next Monday. The Sandinistas are Communists and they are backed by Cuba and Russia. If we don't stop the Sandinistas now, they will keep right on going and take all of Central America.

ANOTHER POINT OF VIEW

The Sandinistas chased the Contras to the border, but they didn't actually invade. They just shot over the border. President Reagan did this to try to get money for the Contras. He shouldn't have sent the paratroopers. How can that little country be a danger to a big country like the United States?

The children could discuss the two columns, defending their positions; the tone is one of debate. A number of children add evidence to their reasoning but need several tries to clarify their positions. Before the discussion peaks (after about thirty minutes, in this instance) the teacher could ask the children to take out their learning journals (a spiral-bound book in which children make various entries for themselves and as directed by the teacher):

TEACHER: Now that we've discussed these two positions I'd like you to take out your journals and write two lines or so about your position. Which one of these two have you decided to take? Or you may not have decided which position yet, which is just fine. Say, "I haven't decided yet and here's why." For those of you who have taken a position, I'd like you to list several reasons why you have taken that stand.

Because the decision to discuss the use of paratroopers was made rather spontaneously, I might ask the children to come to school the next day prepared to support various positions with material from newspapers or evidence from television or any other source they might use to document their stands.

LEARNING JOURNALS
Learning journals are used in many different ways to fit the learning styles of both teachers and students. They can be given many different names, depending on the ages of students and on the ways they evolve most effectively in individual classrooms. Journals are used to record opinions, observations, experiments, facts, experimental thinking, planning, reactions to books read, difficulties encountered, and so on. They are used spontaneously by students, usually under teacher direction. The following are a few specific examples:

- *Experiments by students.* An experiment in describing a character in a piece of fiction initiated by a student, or following a strong recommendation by a teacher. "Marilyn, I'd like you to take five minutes to just describe this new character in your story to see what she looks like." (Journals are a helpful place to keep experiments that may never be used, yet are helpful to students. Teachers often introduce experiments through strong recommendations that students try them in their journals. In this way students will find out new ways for their journals to be used.)
- *Predictions.* Teacher: Okay, I'd like you to predict the outcome of the Honduran event. What do you think the situation will be two weeks from now? Say why if you think you can. (This is also a natural kind of journal entry for science, where observations and hypotheses following observations are an important part of learning to think in that discipline.)
- *Point of view.* Where several points of view exist from

children's discussion about politics, books they have read, plots, characters, or predictions, children can write for two minutes listing the arguments that will be used by the side opposite their own. (This is a more advanced step, to represent the positions of others, yet in each class some children are ready to represent other points of view.)

- *Webbing.* Brainstorm through webbing. (Journals can be used to chart out patterns of thought through webs. It is a quick way to get the "feel" of a subject or idea. See pp. 85 and 88.)
- *Lists:* Lists of things to do, lists of words that are "all about" the same subject, or lists of words the child likes. (Listing is an important element in learning to abstract and can begin very early in school.)
- *Problems solved.* Write a short entry on any learning problems you've solved lately, something you didn't know how to do but do now. (This is one way for children to be more specifically aware of their learning successes and histories.)

The journal gives the student a sense of history as a learner and a place to plan out a future. The range of student sensitivity to the power of learning journals is enormous.

You will want to show how you use your own journal to learn and record your thinking. Write in a spiral-bound book similar to the children's, and from time to time, share your entries. At other times it might be important to show children how you might do an entry on the overhead projector, chalkboard, or experience chart paper.

FURTHER DEVELOPMENT
The Honduras-paratrooper incident allows the teacher several options for encouraging the children's development of a sense of "point of view." (Bear in mind that the options presented here are usually developed from learning episode to learning episode rather than through a single issue.) When children have

demonstrated their ability to record their own positions along with supporting information, I challenge them to try to represent the opposing point of view. This can even be done schematically, point by point. Here, for example, the government point of view is at the left, while another point of view is on the right.

GOVERNMENT VIEW	ANOTHER POINT OF VIEW
1. *The Sandinistas invaded Honduras.*	1. *The Sandinistas shot over the border but didn't actually invade.*
2. *The Sandinistas wanted to severely damage the Contras before the peace meeting the following week.*	2. *The Sandinistas might have wanted to weaken the Contra position, but the Contras have no claim on Nicaragua.*
3. *The Sandinistas are backed by Russia and Cuba.*	3. *It is true that the Sandinistas are backed by Russia and Cuba, but this does not mean there is a big threat.*
4. *If we don't stop the Sandinistas now they will continue to be a threat to all peace-loving countries around them and eventually to us.*	4. *The Sandinistas are just trying to get rid of the Contras, who have raided many of the small towns in Nicaragua, killing many innocent people.*
5. *President Reagan is against Communism and has always fought against it wherever he could.*	5. *The President is still trying to get money for the Contras and this is his way of getting sympathy for them.*
6. *The Contras are freedom fighters.*	6. *The Contras are rascals who just like to fight and want to regain power in Nicaragua.*

Just because other points of view exist, it does not mean that children value them. They may be able to be sensitive to a variety of views in discussing a text or an interpretation of a character in a story, but the political arena, which reflects family values and priorities, may be too difficult to handle. Thus, teachers need to help children understand various points of view, whether in reading, in the creation of characters in fiction, over differences of opinion about how to conduct and organize a classroom, or in various interpretations of political events.

CHILDREN'S LETTERS   A few children will be ready to express their views in a letter. When children write in the learning journals, they are doing sound preliminary work for composing a letter expressing their views to their senator or to another individual with whom they wish to share those views. Writing to one person is different from writing to "the public" in a letter to the editor. Even though the child may not know that one person, writing to an individual is usually easier.

At Stratham Memorial School where we are currently conducting research, one teacher, Barbara Brabson, was concerned that a public letter written by a child often represents the opinions of a parent. She felt that the parent ought to be part of the project. Some parents might object, but others might be delighted and encouraging to teachers who wished to have children share their views. In any event, parents ought to be involved as much as possible. Where appropriate, children could write letters to their parents about their positions, even exchanging written statements. So much depends on the school and community that the teacher has to gauge the best way for children to write about their views. Always in this type of wrestling with real issues in the classroom, the teacher works to help children develop both their own point of view and the ability to state the views of others.

Here are two samples of letters children wrote to senators

that demonstrate how they used the letter form and how they integrated their views about the Honduras issue:

Dear Senator,

My name is John Rezendes and I'm in the fifth grade. We have had a lot of discussions about Honduras and our sending of paratroops there. I want to tell you what I think about it.

I think it was important for us to do it because the Sandinistas have to know they can't keep invading Honduras. That is wrong and we have to stop them.

I wondered what you thought about it. Some people say the President didn't let you know what he was doing but maybe he didn't have time to do that. What do you think?

Thank you for your help.

Sincerely,

In this letter, John Rezendes first identifies or introduces himself to the "stranger," the senator. (Recall that in the letter to the gym teacher, the children first focused on the teacher because both parties knew each other.) John then goes on to identify the issue and why he is writing the letter: to state his opinion. He gives the facts that go with his opinion and then asks the senator for his stance on the question. The letter goes back and forth between "I" and "you," simulating some of the elements in a conversation.

The next letter, by Angela Markham from the same class, is an example of another approach to the topic:

Dear Senator,

I am very upset about the sending of paratroops to Honduras the other day. We did this too quickly without thinking it through. I am letting you know because it is important to let our senators know what we think.

I am a fifth grade student from New Hampshire and we had a long discussion about the problem. Some are with the government. I am not because I think we just keep things stirred up.

*I was wondering what you think about the situation. Would you
let me know? Thank you.*

Sincerely,

Without identifying who she is or where she is from, Angela
moves directly to the task, stating exactly what is on her mind.
Only after her very direct statement does she mention that she
is a fifth-grade student. Like the first student, she wants to find
out what the senator thinks about the situation.

Although letters are conversations—some more distant than
others—it is important to recognize that there is no set way to
write a letter. Through mini-lessons, you can show different
ways in which the same issue or problem can be approached.
On the other hand, remember that showing too many options
can be confusing. Children will find their own ways of trying
different approaches, and these need to be recognized in class.

THE ESSAY   A careful examination of children's ability to state opinions,
express contrary points of view, or write letters filled with information will provide evidence that they are ready to work
with the essay long before it is introduced in most school curricula. Children have so little opportunity to write meaningful
nonfiction that we seldom find out what they are capable of
doing in the nonfiction genre.

When teachers understand how children change as writers
and sense the appropriateness of particular genres for particular
occasions, and when they compose letters and essays themselves, then children will also. The essay makes different demands on the writer, and the context for using them is different
from that of many other forms the child has used up to this
point. Still, teachers ought to sense when the essay will provide
children with an appropriate form of expression.

LOOK FOR ESSAY
OPPORTUNITIES   I am always looking for essay opportunities for myself and for
my students. Essays are both declarations and artful persua-

sions; they teach while drawing on all the best notions we have about how to help others understand our point of view. Unlike narrative, which uses a hierarchical structure and the familiar grammar of the story, the essay changes the usual time–space sequences. The writer creates a reader by way of the "other self," a learner/reader, who needs redundancies not unlike those contained in oral discourse. It is time to show you what I mean. Here is a short essay based on my earlier letter to Senator Rudman.

The Friendly skies look blue but may soon be filled with smoke, fire, and falling debris. Three weeks ago I experienced a near-miss at Logan International Airport in Boston. I became a statistic of the "near-miss," part of that growing body of people who are still alive, yet have been reported as near-participants in disasters. The Federal Aviation Association requires the reports. The reports are frequently investigated. The results of these investigations, however, are seldom made public. I like to fly and I am part of the public. I want to know more.

Eight years ago President Reagan destroyed the Air Traffic Controllers Union. They went on strike complaining that their jobs were stressed; for that kind of stress they wanted more pay. Newspapers publicized their high salaries. For those salaries we figured stress was a necessary hazard. We didn't want to be held hostage by a bunch of guys in a control tower. The president got rid of the union and federalized the positions, bringing in new air traffic controllers from the military and training new persons from the civilian sector.

The air traffic controllers are complaining again, and we need to listen to them. When I left Logan Airport I railed against the controllers who had contributed to our near-miss. On a bright, sunny day our plane, in full, open throttle, aborted at the last moment because it would enter the same airspace as another jet landing at right angles to our own. My sympathies shifted two days later when landing at Stapleton Airport in Denver, Colorado.

I tuned in on my headphones to discussions between our pilots and the control tower in Denver. I counted four commercial flights and one civilian pilot under the direction of our controller. For twenty minutes our controller spoke nonstop, calling directions in rotation to each flight, "United 434, maintain 8000, five degrees right . . . Continental 121, maintain 8000, ten degrees left." In the middle of directions to commercial ships, a voice from the runway was heard, "Hey, y'all, do I take a left on this next runway?" "Y'all" had to be redirected three times before he got the right runway for takeoff.

The burgeoning number of flights, both commercial and private, overrun the already strained capabilities of the air controllers, many of whom have less than five years of service. Logan International Airport has raised fees for private craft to a high level, hoping that most will move to other airports, thus reducing the number of aircraft in the sky at one time and raising the level of flight ability through commerical pilots.

This is a very short essay built on experience, reading, and a review of history from the PATCO strike eight years ago. It was written in about thirty minutes and was rooted in another piece of nonfiction, the letter to Senator Rudman. In fact, the essay is an extension of the letter. The essay contains an interweaving of history, personal narrative, reflection, and commentary, along with an attempt to circle the subject from the point of view of travelers, air controllers, airports, and pilots. The problem is presented immediately. Verbal signals give the reader a sense of the structure of the essay: "Things aren't made public; I am riled enough to find out more facts and share them with you." The history of the problem follows immediately. The details of the near-accident are placed much farther along in the piece than in my letter on the subject and are contained in one sentence: "On a bright, sunny day our plane, in full, open throttle, aborted at the last moment because it would enter the same airspace as another jet landing at right angles to our own."

Points of view shift in the piece because another kind of narrative weaves its way through the piece: the story of the getting of the information. The final paragraph gives more information, not of a personal nature, but about what airports have had to do to deal with the problem. Still, with all of these data, with all the points of view represented in some form, the underlying issue of near-misses has not been resolved. Having just detailed my own experience, I will not return to stress this point. I believe the power of the issue remains in the "unsaid."

Shirley Brice Heath (1987) has done an extensive examination of the history of the essay, tracing its origins in letters and journals. There is an egalitarian notion that goes with the essay: "This is what I think, now what do you think?" seems to be the running idea in the genre. In my own case, I had an experience with a near-miss collision and simply stated my view of the situation, bringing in many other points of view to explain my own. Heath stresses the oral roots of the essay, then traces them back to journals and letters and forward to the essay itself. Her major critique of the way schools handle the essay is that these roots have been disregarded, and the whole notion of what an essay is for has therefore been lost. The essay then becomes an artificial piece of writing composed in the formulaic fashion that is epitomized in the traditional five-paragraph essay.

Heath stresses that there are preliminaries in a learner's profile that are necessary for writing the essay.

- Students must be able to give recounts of experiences supported by their own evidence.
- Students must see themselves as individual knowers. Many cultures socialize people into thinking they have no territory of knowledge. Our own culture socializes women in this way.
- Students must be given opportunities to assert their

expertise over some bodies of knowledge. They need experience in asserting their knowledge.
• Students must be able to focus on how words are used and organized. They must be able to turn the text back on itself and experiment with language and organizations.

The roots of the effective essay, a sense of point of view, and the development of more advanced communication are in strong oral discussion, with the addition of ample opportunity for many types of writing—letters, journal entries, learning logs —done frequently and with audiences who respond to ideas and opinions. When effective communication takes off, the audience broadens beyond the classroom and the school, and the genres follow the contours of children's need. Essays, poems, short stories, personal narratives, debates, directions, all arise from the conditions of literacy set in the classroom. These are dictated by the sensitivity of the teacher to those questions that affect the everyday life of students. Methods that prescribe form are suspect. Form should follow function, and function is determined by the present-tense orientation of literate events.

4

*the lively art of the
interview*

Some time ago I decided to conduct a different kind of workshop. I experimented to see how many resources were within a three-minute walking distance from a school, and then I set up a schedule so the staff would have thirty minutes to interview a person near the school and learn all they could.

One January morning in western New York state, the staff came in prepared for the usual "sit and git" workshop. "Don't take off your coats," I told them, and I passed out sealed envelopes to each team of two persons. "All right, at precisely 9:10, open your envelopes and proceed." A typical set of directions read:

Mr. Karl Kranz, at Kranz Antiques next door to the school, is expecting you to visit at 9:15 in order to learn all you can about bureaus in the American colonies between 1700 and 1730. You have thirty minutes. From 9:45 until 10:15 your team will have a chance to figure out how you will teach what you know to others. Then from 10:15 until 10:45 you will have the opportunity to teach three different groups what you have learned.

My preparation for the workshop had begun two weeks before. I started with Mr. Kranz, the antiques dealer next to the school. I learned that his entire home was a virtual museum, and that each bedroom represented a particular period in colonial America. No one from the school had ever visited him, with the exception of the children who had reclaimed playground balls that had gone over his fence. Mr. Kranz agreed to help with the workshop. I asked him if he knew any other people on the street within a three-minute walking distance of the school who had particular knowledge about something and who would not mind being interviewed.

"Yes, there is a woman across the street in the Methodist church who is an expert on stained glass windows. Mrs. Karl, six doors down the street, has carvings from the Black Forest, or you might interview her about her real expertise, flower arranging. Mrs. Eaton has two-thousand-year-old Chinese tapestries." I found that people who like to learn know other people who also enjoy learning and sharing that learning with others. Before the morning was out, I'd also enlisted the help of the foreman of a building under construction three doors up from the school, a ham radio operator willing to set up a schedule for fifth-grade teachers teaching a unit on Australia, an auto mechanic, and the building custodian, who would explain how the staff might help to save energy. I've since found that most everyone has an area of expertise; the challenge is to find out what it is and allow that person to help others discover what they know.

The focus of the workshop provided a very limited amount of time in which to collect and organize the information the participating teachers would need to share with others, again within a short time. At the end of the workshop, staff members shared their approaches to learning and teaching along with the information they'd discovered. Although I had hoped they would learn about the range of resources so near the school, I hoped even more that they would enjoy the experience of learning from others in a team situation, and in turn, that they would help children to learn from others through interviewing.

The art of interviewing is the art of learning how to learn from other people. It is one of the learner's most important tools for growing and an imperative for the twenty-first century. Yet schools today rarely provide the opportunity to learn the strategies for learning from others. In my day these strategies were called "cheating" or not doing your own work. Well, there is a place to do our own work, but today more than ever, we need more emphasis on learning from people who know things—in just about any way we can. The knowledge explosion is such that textbooks simply cannot deliver the full, rich store of information we need to function effectively in society.

Make no mistake, systematic learning and inquiry remain essential, but the process of learning how to learn, and especially how to learn from others, can no longer be omitted from the school curriculum.

I subscribe to a computer repair service that guarantees that the computer in my home will be in service within eight hours after a problem arises. The service has numerous mobile trucks connected by radio throughout the New England area. I call an 800 number at the central office, they call the truck, and within two or three hours the repair technician has arrived to go to work. It surprised me to find out that the person who appears is prepared and usually equipped to service forty to fifty different makes of computers. He doesn't actually know everything about all those computers, but he does know who to call for help.

I observed the network in operation as he made a series of calls, jumping from person to person, interviewing them, helping them teach him how to service my more obscure and ancient computer. It was clear to me that this man carried branching trees of informants in his head with telephone numbers to match. There was a delight to his work—he renewed contacts with friends he hadn't called for a while as he added to his basic knowledge about computers the more refined expertise of others. Problems with difficult computers like my own were opportunities for further learning rather than frustrating dead-ends for a person without contacts.

The learner of tomorrow is going to have to know how to function through networks of people who all together constitute an efficient and effective cooperative information community. We must begin today to help ourselves and our children become conscious of learning how to learn and of how to teach others to help us learn. The classroom community must change to meet this challenge.

You have already helped prepare children to conduct inter-views because you may have already done many of the follow-ing:

- *Writing and reading conferences.* Children are used to participating in whole-class sharing of books and writing. They are used to *focusing on the person* who shares.
- *Sequence of questions.* Children are used to initiating and sequencing questions to achieve meaning. If teachers ask most of the questions, children will not grow in their ability to ask more than one question at a time.
- *Point of view.* Children have been prepared to state both their own point of view and the points of view of others. Sensitivity to other points of view depends on an awareness of one's own point of view. Both are needed in interviewing.
- *Notetaking.* Children have had some help with notetaking, although much more help will be needed.
- *Survey interviews.* Children have already participated in short-term interviews of a classroom-polling type (see Chapter 2).
- *Help structures.* The classroom already encourages cooperative learning. When children are stuck, they can ask others for help. When children take on new classroom jobs, they are teamed with someone who is experienced in order to learn from and with that person. The classroom tone suggests that it is all right not to know and that there are many options for learning to learn from others.
- *Need for information.* The classroom needs information in order to function well. Children compile information books because these are needed in content areas. Interviews are collated and published under the rubric "Classroom Opinions." Questions arise, big questions that require reading and gathering information. A broad base of information is required in order to create a learning community.

ACTION: CONDUCT AN INTERVIEW.

Conduct an interview with another adult. I strongly suggest that you work with a team member who is willing to learn with you as you work through this chapter on interviewing together. See what you can learn about something that that person knows in ten minutes. When you have finished your interview, then reverse the procedure and ask your colleague to interview you. Both procedures will be important.

If you don't have a colleague to interview, then choose a family member or anyone you know who has specific knowledge about something. I went into the living room where my wife, Betty, was reading the paper and asked for a ten-minute interview. Fortunately, she was at a point where she could talk with me:

DON: I'd like to interview you about something you know that I know nothing about.

BETTY: All right, you haven't been to El Rosario in Honduras. Ask me about that. [*Betty had just returned from a two-week work session at a medical mission in rural Honduras. I have only fleeting knowledge about the village.*].

DON: How did the group happen to go to El Rosario?

BETTY: It was really out of our hands. It was chosen by IACHI [*the church group from Honduras coordinating mission work*].

DON: Well, why did IACHI choose El Rosario as the place to go then?

BETTY: It is a sort of central town in the midst of other towns. You go about forty-five minutes up a bumpy road into the mountains to get there. It is in the middle of a lot of other small villages. There are only four hundred people living there. They have a coffee-growing cooperative.

DON: How did they get the coffee-growing cooperative started?

BETTY: Maybe through the church group. They have a model

agricultural farm called Protozona; that's what it's called. They have fruit trees, crops, mangos, avocados.

DON: Does IACHI develop markets too?

BETTY: I'm not sure what they do on that.

DON: As you go into the village, what strikes you?

BETTY: Two things. The poverty. It is run-down. It is messy. Paper and plastic thrown away, and running water at the edge of the streets filled with animal manure, and it is green and slimy. But [there is] great interest in what the gringos are doing. I am struck by the friendliness and the sharing of what they have. I am struck by the children.

DON: Say something about the children.

BETTY: Adults and children are the same. The children are even more open. They are trusting. They have so little. There are no toys. They are so responsive. They are super-interested in every little thing the gringos are doing. What we do is entertainment for them—day or night. They are like a blank page waiting to be filled.

DON: Do the children play?

BETTY: Yes, of course, simple games with stones on the ground. But there are no toys. All the time I was there I only saw one small block of wood with wheels on it. That was the only toy.

Children work. They do simple chores all day long. They gather firewood, babysit, get corn, take corn to be ground. They are always going to get water, going to the one general store, getting cows or some animal out of the beans; they herd cattle, ride horseback; there is a saying, "Everything is hard in Honduras." There are no mechanical aids at all and everything takes a long time; even washing your hands takes a lot longer.

Many go to school. School hours are long.

DON: How long and how often do they go?

BETTY: From 8:00 A.M. until 4:00 P.M., five days a week.

DON: Sounds like there are an awful lot of chores to do in that village.

BETTY: Yup. And the children pick wild fruits. They also get the stiff ends of bushes to make into brush ends and make brooms.

I saw one family where three or four children were in a hammock swinging and singing the national anthem they'd learned in school. I saw little circle games they'd probably learned at school.

DON: Ten minutes is up. Thanks, I learned a lot about El Rosario. I had no idea how much the children in a village like that had to do.

The interview, like the conference, is based on the last bit of information someone tells you. As I look back over my ten-minute transcript I notice that I began with a story kind of question: "How did the group happen to go to El Rosario?" Betty gave a little information, but it still didn't go very far. I pushed with another question. In fact, I pushed with a series of additional questions that probed for a story that might give some history, and some sense of origins: "Why did IACHI choose El Rosario as the place to go then?" and "How did they get the coffee-growing cooperative started?" I don't think these questions interested Betty very much. They were part of my own agenda, and I didn't sense the story or the information Betty wanted to tell me about her subject. Not until I asked, "As you go into the village, what strikes you?" Now she could tell her story and really teach me about what she knew, especially about the children in the village. Telling about the children was new ground—for both of us. Interviews take off when both participants realize both are learning at the same time. Getting to that point requires listening to the information the informant speaks, but it also requires a realization on the part of the informant that the new information is affecting the person conducting the interview.

Subsequent to writing my analysis I asked Betty about her impressions of the interview. She confirmed some of my analysis, and more.

BETTY: When you asked me those early questions I thought to myself, "Oh, I don't care anything about that. He must be thinking I don't know anything about El Rosario." I wondered if the interview would ever amount to anything. I thought, "Those were good questions and maybe I should have spent more time learning about them."

Those were thoughts I wish she hadn't had. I wish I had gotten off my own agenda and on to hers more quickly. The point of any interview is not what an informant should know as much as what that person *does* know.

ACTION: BE INTERVIEWED.

Reverse the process and ask your colleague to interview you about something you know that will probably be new information for him or her. Even if the person already knows something about your subject, it is unimportant. The essential element in the interview is what you know about the subject that is important to you. After the interview is over, think through some of these questions:

- When were you (the person interviewed) most interested in the content you were sharing? Ask your partner if he/she could tell and why.
- When was it easiest for you to speak? Why was it easier for you to speak at that point?
- What do you wish you'd been asked?

Share some of your observations with the person who interviewed you. The last question listed above—"What do you wish you'd been asked?"—is traditionally covered in interviews in one final question: "Is there anything else you'd like to say that you haven't said yet?" (I was sticking to the ten-minute deadline and didn't allow enough time for this question in my interview.) One final point: When you are interviewed, you will learn as much about what works as if you'd conducted the interview yourself.

Enjoy learning what you didn't know you knew.

ACTION: INTRODUCE CHILDREN TO THE INTERVIEW.

Children can interview you about something you know so that when the story unfolds, it will be of interest to them. I often use an object that is important to me and that has some significance in the story. But when I answer their questions I give only the information framed by the question. I want them to find out what kind of information is elicited by what kind of question.

Once the interview is over, I am interested in what they have learned about the object and the knowledge that goes with it, about me, and about what questions brought out good information. A fourth question that can be used with more advanced students is: What did you learn about yourself during the interview? This is information that has nothing to do with what they have said. It just gets triggered. It might be a feeling or a "that reminds me" kind of thing.

Here is an example of an interview some children did with me. I had brought in a six-inch-long sperm whale's tooth for them to ask about.

DON: I have something here that is important to me. See how much you can learn about the object and me along with it. You ask questions and I'll answer them.

CHILD: What is it?

DON: A tooth.

CHILD: What kind of a tooth?

DON: A whale's tooth.

CHILD: What kind of a whale?

DON: A sperm whale.

CHILD: How did you get it?

DON: Oh, that's quite a story. I was visiting two old women who were sisters. I guess they were maybe in their eighties, maybe even their nineties. And they were all cramped into their tiny rooms with hardly any place to go or sit. This was about twenty-five years ago. I was sitting there and one of them said, "We've got some things we think are valuable, some lovely shells from the South Pacific. Do you think someone might like to buy them?" "Oh, I don't know," I said. "Let's take a look." She went into the other room and came out with a white box wrapped in string. She opened the box and there were shells all right, beautiful shells, much the same as I had at home from my great-great-grandfather. But shells are shells. Old or new they aren't worth much. But over in the corner of the box were two objects, and when I picked them up they turned out to be this tooth and one other.

"Oh," I said, "these shells aren't worth much, but these teeth are. If you are interested, I'll ask someone who knows how much they are worth, and if I can afford it, I'll buy them."

So, I could afford them and I bought them from the two ladies. What else would you like to know?

CHILD: How much did you pay for them?

DON: I'm not sure, but I think it was something like eighty dollars.

CHILD: What's that stuff on the sides? It looks like a picture.

DON: It is a picture taken from an old magazine that they copied on to here. It is a picture of an Indian, though it doesn't look much like one.

CHILD: It sure doesn't.

CHILD: Do you like it?

DON: Yes.

CHILD: Why do you like it?

DON: Well, my great-great-grandfather was a whaler. This tooth was given to one of the old ladies I bought it from.

The man's name was Brownell, and he sailed from New Bedford, the same place my great-great-grandfather sailed from. He told this woman when she was about ten years old that he'd bring her back a tooth from his voyage of hunting whales, and he did. It was kind of a nice story and I imagined that my great-great-grandfather would have done the same for me. Sometimes you can make up stories about things you like, and it makes the thing special.

After the interview we discussed what worked, what didn't work, and which questions brought the most information. I told them that I could give more information when their questions probed into "how" and "why," and that I could connect myself better with the information. The latter was more difficult for them to see as valuable, although possibly their own experiences will come to help them understand. And that is the next Action.

ACTION: INTERVIEW A CHILD.

Children need to be interviewed for the same reasons adults do. They need to experience what they will practice with others, to feel the flow of information coming from themselves in front of the class—just as they do when the class interviews them about their reading and writing. During the interview, you try to demonstrate what the child knows and how she knows it. It may be useful to have a child use an object to help with the interview, although with older students (grades 4–6) this may not be necessary at all. Interviews don't need to be conducted with every child in the room; rather, they are practiced periodically to help certain children "know what they know" before a group and to demonstrate various approaches to interviews.

ACTION: USE PREFERENTIAL POLLS AS BACKGROUND FOR THE INTERVIEW.

In Chapter 2 I talked about preferential polling as a way of introducing the interview and of developing an understanding of the idea of "point of view." In the next phase of interviewing, children move on to try to find out the basis for the thinking behind the polling data. Here are some examples of preferential polling for upper-grade children:

- Favorite foods.
- Favorite athletic teams.
- Favorite animals.
- Favorite songs.
- Favorite television programs.
- Favorite authors.
- Favorite books.
- Other polls designed by children.

Let us suppose that when a poll about favorite animals was conducted in fifth grade, the following data were accumulated:

- Horses: 10
- Dogs: 8
- Cats: 5
- Snakes: 2

In a class of twenty-five children, ten voted for horses, and two voted for snakes. The next task is to interview these children about the reasons for their choices. In this way, the data behind the numbers will be revealed. (When children are interviewed, they have a right to give no reasons. In fact, they have a right to say they don't even want to select an animal. Children have a right to privacy in the classroom as they do later, as adult citizens.)

For children who wish to be interviewed, demonstrate how you find out about the information that underlies their choices. The approach is a simple one:

TEACHER: Which choice did you make?
CHILD: Horses.
TEACHER: Tell me about your choice.

CHILD: I've always liked horses. My grandfather had one once, and he let me sit on him. We'll never have one, but I like them, that's all.

TEACHER: Thank you. Is there anything else you'd like to say about your choice?

CHILD: No, I think that's it.

Interviews for polling are rarely complex; children simply give their reasons. Yet the focus of the poll is shaped by the simple choices they make. Children will be able to see how a single choice can result in a complex range of responses. Just what stands behind a vote will be quite obvious. A number of findings can emerge from these polls:

- Children who choose dogs may have more details in their reasoning than children who choose horses.
- Children may have little experience with horses and far more with cats than dogs.
- Girls may choose horses. Boys choose dogs.

Of course, children could also formulate questions they wished to examine to find out "how come they voted that way." Children may also discover several points of view about why horses were chosen as most popular.

Polling within classrooms results in data that can be included in collections of information about the class. If used effectively, polling can help children begin to identify the similarities and differences within the classroom. The nature of consensus and individual difference is portrayed for all to see. Subtle and systematic work on the beauty of differences, however, requires teacher sensitivity to build a classroom community.

ACTION: CONDUCT MINI-LESSONS ON NOTETAKING.

If children are to be able to work with data from interviews, they will need to know how to take notes. Use the overhead projector as you conduct an interview with one of the children.

For example, when I interviewed the child about her reason for choosing horses, I wrote:

STATEMENT	NOTES
I've always liked horses.	*like horses*
My grandfather had one once,	*grandfather had one*
and he let me sit on him.	*sat on him*
We'll never have one, but I	*never have one*
like them, that's all.	*like them*

Notetaking involves putting down essential information, abstracting agent and action ("like horses"). Children can practice doing this at their seats while you write on a piece of paper, then transfer the paper to an overhead. This can be an effective mini-lesson that will take no more than a few minutes. How hard it is to conduct an interview and write at the same time, but the focus of an interview, especially an interview involving several people on the same subject, should clarify the process of notetaking.

ACTION: BRING PEOPLE IN FOR INTERVIEWING.

When about a third of the children have demonstrated that they are able to interview, bring in a guest. I suggest a guest from the school—another faculty member, someone from the cafeteria, or the custodian. Do a preliminary interview with the guest:

TEACHER: I would like my children to have some experience in interviewing people from outside of the classroom. Choose an area, or an experience that has happened to you, a place you've been or something you know how to do that has little to do with school in the formal sense. If you have some object or material that would give a focus to the interview, that might be helpful.

There are two routes that this kind of interview can take. It can be done with the whole class, as when I was interviewed about my whale's tooth. Another exciting route is the "scoop" approach, which requires more time from the person being interviewed, about an hour. While the rest of the children go about their regular work, teams of three children each interview the guest at ten-minute intervals. Eventually the whole class participates, depending on how long the visitor can stay. If possible, work in the hall or another small room, which heightens the sense of a possible "scoop" as well as the importance of the session. (The children should already have learned a little about the topic through advance reading from sources suggested by the guest expert.) They then quietly interview the person to get good information and perhaps some "scoop" the other teams may not acquire. A scoop usually relates to the personal relationship the interviewee has with his or her subject. The children write up their interviews and, when all have completed their pieces, share them at one time. This approach heightens the importance of effective notetaking, advance preparation, and interesting writing.

Interviews with an entire class limit the number of questions any one child may be able to ask during one single interview. The team approach allows children to sequence questions and build on prior information to get the needed scoop.

A KEY STEP One of the most challenging aspects of any interview is the point at which questions are based on information the guest has just given the interviewer. One of the difficult elements in preparing children with questions and reading is the "fill-in" aspect of an interview. Children fill in the blanks to their questions but ignore more important information the guest has to share. Going back over my own interview with my wife, Betty, I notice that I wasn't listening to the story she wished to tell. Although I built my interview on a little prior information, I needed a simpler question: "What struck you?" In short, I had my own blanks. Our role as professionals in this instance and throughout the course of our work with children on conducting interviews is to point out effective questions that release information, to help children see when their questions have worked. Data about effective questions can be shared by both the person interviewed and the team or class conducting the interview.

INTERVIEWS ACROSS THE CURRICULUM

Interviews work well across the curriculum. In almost every community, someone has traveled to the very country the class may be studying. You can make the subject live by having people share their stories and their own personal reactions to the countries in which they have traveled. When I followed up leads for my workshop on the streets near the school in western New York state, I uncovered people who had traveled to China, Italy, and several countries in South America. Best of all, the ham radio operator set up a schedule so that children could participate in acquiring information about Australia from Australians themselves. Later, he went on to set up interviews for the children in other areas of geographical and historical interest.

The local community includes computer experts and programmers, and people who have had unusual experiences. Once it is known that a local school wants to learn from and build on community resources, all manner of persons come forward to recommend others who can contribute to children's learning. As principal, I used to maintain lists of people who were willing to help with the school curriculum. The librarian also assisted in maintaining lists, with parental support. Note, however, that people are not asked to come in to give speeches or present slide shows. (In the long run, this also makes it easy to recruit people to help.) Too many envision themselves pinned against the wall by unruly children. Rather, the children do the work, learning through preparation and careful questioning what people in their school and community have to teach them. The Foxfire project is an inspiring example of how a school can capitalize on local resources through interviews with townspeople who have stories to tell about themselves and their community.

Books, newspapers, and periodicals are more interesting to read when a local author or expert has gone over the information and pointed the children in the direction of new resources. It is the mixture of the live event with print materials that makes learning exciting.

Other resources for interviewing and building effective human resources through the curriculum are those children who have composed important formal reports. (See Chapter 5.) They ought to be well prepared for interviews through their knowledge of both materials and information.

USE THE TELEPHONE   Another effective approach to interviewing is the telephone conference call to interviewees who are farther away. By using a speaker phone that can be placed in the center of the classroom, children can interview people in their offices in local, state, and national government. Scientists, authors, and university experts are all a letter or telephone call away through specific arrangements. Cost is involved, but the school can invest in a permanent speaker phone, and the charge for a long distance call is not that high, even in prime school time. The local parent-teacher group might help with costs, or even room funds could be used to demonstrate just how useful such approaches can be. Once the power of this approach has been demonstrated, funds are not that difficult to acquire in most communities.

Gathering information by telephone is more abstract and therefore more difficult than when the person is actually present in the classroom. Before attempting telephone interviews, children ought to have considerable experience. Trying an interview through a local telephone conference call is probably a good way to begin.

FINAL REFLECTIONS   In this country we are preoccupied with print, so much so that living, human resources—people who are full of information—are neglected as informants within most school curricula. Even more neglected is the lively art of interviewing people so that we learn not only what they know, but how they have acquired that information. In our schools we fail to explore the human dimensions of learning. We study Cape Cod, for example, but seldom talk with someone who has lived or traveled there. Australia is an island continent about which we acquire stereotypical notions of crocodiles (from *Crocodile Dundee*), kangaroos, and koala bears. But it is possible to talk with people who live there and find out firsthand their own notions of what life is like down under. Again, we may know something about tide pools but seldom share in the natural enthusiasm of the biologist in the process of discovering, or hear about how scientists study and work in relation to their subjects. Through interviews we learn how to ask questions that open the door to connecting the person with his or her work. "How did you happen to get interested in tide pools, Dr. Walker?"

The thinker/learner/worker of tomorrow can no longer remain in isolated ignorance. Problems are opportunities for contacting the person who knows. We can work as far as we can, formulating effective questions as we encounter difficulties, but then we will make the phone call. The 800 service number of the future will be far more specialized than it is today. Students of the future will have to know how to help someone else teach them—informing them of what they understand and then returning with further questions about puzzling information. "I don't understand" will be the three most important words in their learning kit. We are witnessing a rapid explosion of technology and information that brings with it opportunities for the learning tree of informants to graft learning communities together in new and exciting ways. But those trees need to be planted now—and in far different classroom communities than we have seen to date.

5

formal reporting

Nicole wished to write about eagles. The notion that they were an endangered species piqued her curiosity. "You mean they could all be gone some day?" she asked. A discussion stirred among several other children in her second-grade classroom. Leslie Funkhouser, their classroom teacher, joined in. The class identified other endangered species, and about ten children adopted them, intending to read and then write about them.

Up to this point, most of the children wrote primarily in personal narrative, recounting stories that had happened to them. Occasionally they'd write fiction, but most of their writing was in narrative form. When they decided to write about endangered species, it meant a shift in using time and in the tools needed for composing, and new kinds of help from the teacher.

The children also experienced a new notion of literacy. Now they needed to gather information to learn more about their subjects. They didn't write immediately because they needed to read first. Some kept journals and recorded information, just as they had when they responded to their trade books. Others simply read and talked over their discoveries with friends. They also learned that other children in the room possessed knowledge that was useful to them, and that several books and sources of information were available to go with their writing.

Leslie allowed the children to use time differently for their endangered species investigations. Because children put reading and writing to work, the more formal "reading and writing time" disappeared. Furthermore, most of the children sustained their study for at least two weeks and some for three, using the entire language time block, while their teacher helped them with the various skills necessary for successful reporting. The children needed help with understanding their subject, finding sources of information, recording information and organizing it, and sounding like themselves when they wrote. They discovered different points of view—in their sources and in the reactions of their classmates—about how endangered their choice of species was.

Although all reading and writing are demonstrations of meaning negotiated with the world, when children put reading and writing to work to deal with sources beyond the self, they move into a new territory for learning. The self is extended in a new way when reading and writing "go to work."

START MORE FORMAL
REPORTING WITH
CHILDREN

This chapter is meant to help children from about third grade on. Naturally, there are some children in first or second grade who are capable of some formal reporting. Nevertheless, it is important for children to maintain their interest during what for some will seem a rather lengthy operation. What follows is a series of approaches for guiding children through the process. My intent is to help children maintain interest and write a report that sounds like the child who wrote it. I am including more recommendations than are probably healthy for any one child. It will be up to you, as a professional, to decide what works best for individual children in your class. You will know what helps most by observing the children in the process of learning about their subject.

You may find it helpful to begin report writing with just a few children at a time. (Leslie Funkhouser worked with only the ten children who wanted to do reports on endangered species.) When children with strong interests pursue their reporting successfully, their enthusiasm carries over to other class members and inspires future reports.

Children begin more formal reporting the same way they began personal narrative when they first started to write: they choose topics they know something about or topics that have high interest for them. It is much easier to help children learn the process of reporting if they already have some conceptual understanding of the material they will study further. Combining the process of gathering material, abstracting it in notes, organizing the information, and finally writing the report in a voice that sounds like the writer is too tall an order when the concepts contained in the new study are themselves as new as the process.

Children learn to write in the same way. They usually write personal narratives in which the content is merely a recall of events that have happened to them. When children are only recalling the content they already know, the teacher can help them with this process, as with the spelling of words, the notion of audience, and the organization of the material. Early fiction writing can present some of the same problems as reporting: the child engages in pure invention (if the subject is far afield of personal experience), and the fiction process itself becomes a stumbling block. In this instance, the child knows neither the process nor the content.

The approach to more formal reporting in the Actions in this chapter will begin with the exploration of what you and the writer know. Younger students in the primary years are more confident about what they know than older students. It doesn't mean that they do know more than older students, only that they haven't been through the usual school socialization process, which fails to help children establish what they already know at each succeeding grade level. Report writing of the type I am discussing here attempts to establish turf, a sense of what the child knows and controls, and solid content that allows the child's own voice to emerge from the material.

CONTROLLING LENGTH Children's first formal reports should be short. One to one-and-one-half pages is enough space in which to learn how to handle information. Most students fail to learn how to do reports because they are trying to write too much. Filling pages causes children to throw in material that has little to do with their subject. It is not uncommon in some schools to see children trying to write five- to eight-page reports, a length that may even cause problems for college students. Such projects give rise to students' copying from encyclopedias, lacking focus and control of the topic, and using extraneous information.

Even if you do not assign a prohibitive number of pages for the report, some children will write a piece that is too long anyway, because the idea that "longer is better" is pervasive in our culture. (The length syndrome lasts through doctoral dissertations.)

First reports, therefore, ought to be short. There are a number of advantages:

- The student should not strain for information. Rather, the student should be writing from an abundance of information, even to the point of excluding some. If children write with an abundance of information they will have to listen to their material in order to know what to keep.
- When the steps in working with a report fall more closely together, the child can gain an overview of the entire process and its application to the next report.
- Keeping the report short enables the teacher to observe how the child is handling the subject.
- More emphasis can be placed on discovering a subject and finding an area of information that has both high interest and good sources.
- More emphasis can be placed on the process of collecting information and giving the subject some focus.
- The process of helping a child organize information toward meaning, one of the more frequently neglected steps in reporting, can be better developed by working with a small amount of material rather than too much material gathered over several weeks.

There are obviously some children who will be able to handle a longer report, while some who will strain to expand their data to fill a page. This means that some reports will need contraction and others expansion. There is nothing magical about one-and-a-half pages. It is merely a guideline for helping children learn how to write reports without struggling with the burden of length.

ACTION: EXPLORE AREAS OF SELF-KNOWLEDGE WITH CHILDREN.

I suggest working with small clusters of children (a maximum of eight). I try to choose areas of potential interest to children and to me:

DON: I'm going to choose some areas that I sort of know something about but I'd like to know still more about them. I'll jot a few of them down here, then say a little about each.

Cross-country skiing

I've always been interested in sports. Cross-country skiing is a new one. Right now I'm trying to learn more about how to skate, which is a particular way of cross-country skiing. I'm not very good at it, but I'd like to learn more about cross-country skiing itself, some of the history, as well as to get myself ready for the Olympics, which are coming up in a few weeks. Maybe if I know some of the competitors and techniques, I'll be more knowledgeable when it comes on.

Whales

My great-great-grandfather was a whaler and I've read a fair amount about both the history of whales and whale biology, that is, all about how they live and are put together. They are so big, and we know so little about how intelligent they are, how deep they swim. That's the part I think I'd like to learn more about.

Birds

I've had bird feeders for quite some time now, and I'm not very happy with the results. I feed them all right but I don't get the birds I used to. For example, I get chickadees and finches but nothing on the ground. I'd like to learn a lot more about feeding birds. I already know how to identify them pretty well, but where to go from there I don't really know.

The notion of sharing what you know something about should be done in a few sentences. This is not a time to display what you know as much as it is a very brief introduction to bring in some item of interest along with a few facts you have on hand or have read. You may wish to leave out the part about what you want to learn next. It may be enough just to share what you know how to do, or your general knowledge about one specific interest. Then ask the children, "Would you like to share one of your interests or something you know a little bit about?" Bring in your other topics if you think it will help further discussion. From the beginning, oral discussion, the chance to talk about the chosen subject, will be essential to effective composing. This is where the child's voice gets into the piece. The child's sense of authority and knowledge about the subject, so connected with voice, can't start early enough.

ACTION: LOOK AT WHAT YOU KNOW.

After the discussion within the group, I'll start to illustrate my knowledge with a *web*. I'll do this on an overhead, experience chart paper, or the chalkboard.

DON: I've decided to choose the whales. I know a little bit more about whales than the other two. Besides, I'm just more interested in them right now. First, I'll write "Whales" sort of in the center here and then I'll branch out with things that strike me. [*See Figure 5–1.*]

I wonder how deep they'll go. I heard once that a sperm whale got caught on an undersea cable about a mile down on the bottom. Oh, here's one I hadn't thought about at

FIGURE 5–1   A WEB

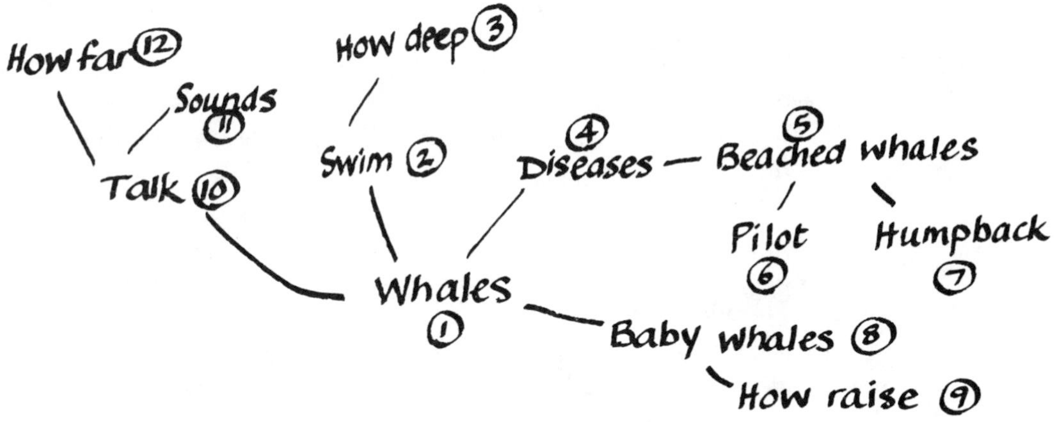

all, diseases. Maybe you've heard or seen on TV the part where pilot whales and then humpback whales were washing up on the beach. That's one to think about.

Then there's baby whales. They are huge when they are born. I've wondered how they are born and how they are raised.

Whales communicate too. They make strange sounds and they travel a long way. Some believe they can talk. That's another thing to think about.

I'd like you to try to think about your topics and make a web. Make branches and put anything you know about them on your chart.

Some children may not work very well with webbing. A few may find that making a list of those words that come to mind when they think about their subjects is more effective. Others may need to draw, to see their subject, and then follow that with words.

The web is one of the earliest ways of showing children how to represent facts or whole areas of learning with single words. The word *diseases* stands for an entire area of learning, *beached whales* for whales that have driven themselves ashore or died at sea to wash ashore. When a child sees that a word or phrase can stand for a whole story or idea, notetaking has begun. It is a useful skill to know, yet it may be difficult for some children to acquire.

ACTION: EXPLORE THE WEB.

Depending on the richness of the web, or what stands behind the words, children may need to narrow or expand the focus in selecting their subject. The guideline is to have enough information yet have a topic that the child still feels worth pursuing. Maintaining this balance is one of the teacher's greatest challenges.

ACTION: FORMULATE QUESTIONS.

I demonstrate how to formulate questions by first showing how I choose a topic from my web. I try to combine information with interest in demonstrating my choice.

DON: I'm not sure I'll do the beached whales or the one on whales communicating with each other. In the last three years, forty or so pilot whales have washed up on the Cape Cod beaches, and no one knows why. Actually, they've been alive when they swim ashore and then they die when the tide goes out. People who like whales go to the beach where they are coming in and try to steer them out to sea, but as soon as they do, they swim right back and die on the beaches. Then the humpback whales have been coming ashore dead, and they suspect it is what they are eating, some chemical change in what they eat.

   The other one that has interested me is how whales communicate. Like the humpback has a song that only other whales in their pod know. It changes just a little bit each year and all the whales put in the change. Then the sperm whales send out these deep low sounds that scientists think can go about a thousand miles. Both of these choices are things I'd like to know more about. I'd say they were a tossup. Which one would interest you if I were to choose it?

If the decision is a toss-up for me, I like to have the children choose with me. In this way, they can participate in my study and in the kinds of decisions I'll make as I do my report. After the children and I have chosen the topic—in this case, "how whales communicate"—I then continue with the next step, the *question web*. Figure 5–2 shows how I prepare myself for reading, talking, and thinking about my subject:

DON: Before I start to gather information and learn more about how whales communicate, I try to think of some

FIGURE 5–2   A QUESTION WEB

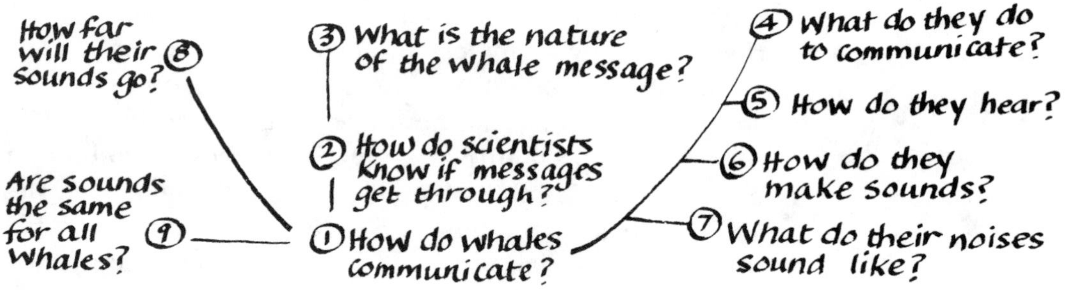

How far will their sounds go? ⑧

③ What is the nature of the whale message?

④ What do they do to communicate?

⑤ How do they hear?

② How do scientists know if messages get through?

⑥ How do they make sounds?

Are sounds the same for all whales? ⑨

① How do whales communicate?

⑦ What do their noises sound like?

questions I probably need to be ready to answer to really find out what I want. So, I'll start here in the center of my paper and write a kind of title: "How do whales communicate?"

I was able to formulate the questions in my question web because of some vague recollection of what I'd read in the past. Most questions come from what we already know. In part, the question always knows its own answer. The beginning of the answer, an understanding of the information, is contained in the formulation of the question. If a child was to begin research on the same subject, she might have questions as general as "How do they communicate?" "How far can they communicate?" "How can they hear each other?"

Three to five questions would be enough to start. Some children may have to do some preliminary reading in order to form some questions that will point them toward more information. A question is a way of organizing information.

Some children will find it helpful to put each question on a single piece of paper. Then, when they are reading, they can simply post the information they discover under the relevant question. They may also formulate new questions during their reading that ought to have their own, separate piece of paper. The learning principle is to have just enough of a notion of a subject, with the right proportion of questions, to help the child to be an active reader. The question-learning load the child can handle is dependent on the richness of children's prior knowledge, their ability to understand the power of the question, and their interest in their choice. It is to be expected that there will be differences between what children include in their first and second webs. You can work with those differences, encouraging children who have many questions and helping those who have only a few.

From time to time, schedule a group session and ask the children to share how they are going about their reports. They will know about sources of information and books that have been helpful, and they can share with each other what helped them. If you are in doubt about some procedures, after the children have done the work ask them what helped and what didn't. If they think you really want to know, they'll tell you.

Some children have to do two or three formal reports before they sense how to choose a subject and how to formulate effective questions. There is no need to rush to help children succeed. Rather, a tone of discovery, sharing in community, and a sense of wonder about the information is what the teacher seeks to foster in the children. The process of learning how to learn—to formulate questions, read, and find an area of knowledge unique to yourself—eludes a majority of students over a lifetime.

ACTION: WORK WITH PICTURE BOOKS.

Picture books are a good place for children to begin to explore their subject. Authors of picture books, if there are any in the child's interest area, have chosen essential information underlying basic concepts. They have often touched on the most elemental areas and introduced broad, general knowledge related to the child's interest area. Some teachers may reason, "Why, this is easy reading; the children should be challenged." But there will be time enough for challenge. What all readers and writers need, at any age, is direct access to well-chosen information.

The information in picture books is usually put together by topflight writers who know their subject just as well as the authors of information books for older students. The difference is that their information is more fundamental and more carefully chosen to coordinate ideas with text and illustrations. The illustrations also serve to encourage understanding of the broader concepts surrounding a subject. For example, my chosen subject is "how whales communicate." I suspect that specific information about communication probably won't find its way into a picture book, yet a fast reading of several picture books will orient me to general knowledge about whales that, in turn, may open up some new questions.

In researching my topic, I read the picture book *The Blue Whale* by Donna K. Grosvenor and Larry Foster (1977), which was published by the National Geographic Society for "Young Explorers." Although the book does not provide material about communication, it does show the life cycle of the blue whale and includes excellent information about my second choice, baby whales. I almost switched. In fact, children may find a quick reading of picture books an excellent way to open up topical areas in their subject for alternative approaches.

The Life of Sea Mammals, a Macdonald Education book (1974), gives even broader background about whales, because it examines them in the context of other sea mammals that once lived on land. It is halfway between a picture book and a regular text and provides numerous illustrations, but of a more technical nature.

Another text, *Whales—Friendly Dolphins and Mighty Giants of the Sea* by Jane Watson (1975) provides some good illustrations, although it is not a picture book, and served to move me into my subject on whale communication. Picture books and their first cousins, information books, which provide more text and good illustrations, can be the basis for an important mini-lesson on the next step in the process of more formal reporting: note-taking.

BASIC GUIDELINE When children are first moving into more formal report writing, it is important for them to become conversationally acquainted with their subject. This means that short five- or ten-minute conversations in which children talk about their sources, have them received by their friends, and are questioned about their content is a valuable way of establishing both voice and authority early on. You will notice that many opportunities for discussion are mentioned here, and you will probably see other, more beneficial areas for the children to discuss. Discussion is rooted in children's ability to listen and question, which this text is meant to help develop.

ACTION: BEGIN TO TAKE NOTES—A MINI-LESSON

Notetaking is one of the most important tools in the student's thinking repertoire. It is also one of the most difficult to learn. Yet there are ways to work with notetaking, beginning with very young children in first and second grade. (Some of these approaches have already been mentioned in Chapter 2, "Informal Reporting.") It is not uncommon to find students entering college who are unable to "take notes." They can only copy complete sentences instead of abstracting or writing a précis.

A note is an abstract of a text written or spoken by another person. It can be an idea that comes in the midst of thinking about a subject. We jot it down, not in complete sentences but in a few words that stand for the whole idea.

Here is a text on "whale communication" that I will quote (Watson, 1975) and then demonstrate ways of abstracting with children (underlining added):

Whales <u>seem to talk</u> to one another. They <u>do not have vocal cords</u> that vibrate when air comes up from the lungs, as humans do. So their <u>sounds</u> are <u>not</u> just <u>like</u> those of <u>human beings</u>. But whales do make different sounds. To people who have listened carefully, some whale <u>sounds seem like squeaks and squeals, squawks and hums. Others like whistles and whines. And some like rich musical tones.</u>

Some whales give a wild sort of a <u>cry when</u> they are <u>unhappy or in trouble</u>. Others "speak" in a <u>language of clicks</u>. Baby whales soon learn to click like the adults. If you could listen to them carefully, you would find that they <u>take turns in "speaking."</u> Surely they must be carrying on some sort of conversation!

DON: I have underlined what I think are the most important words from the book. These are the words that have the most important facts. I'm going to take them out and write them down here; then I will see if I can use them to talk about what I've learned.

seem to talk
do not have vocal cords
sounds not like human beings
sounds like squeaks, squeals, squawks, hums, whistles, whines,
    rich musical tones
cry when unhappy or in trouble
language of clicks
take turns in "speaking"

Notice that I'm writing down just a few words so that I can do this quickly. At the same time, I want to have enough down so that I can remember what those few words stand for. Take a few paragraphs now from your books and put down a few words you think carry the most important information.

Circulate through the group to see how the children select their words and whether their notes carry essential information. Ask questions: "Tell me what idea that information stands for."

Another way of keeping notes is to record the data, the words and phrases, underneath the questions from the question web:

WHAT DO THEIR NOISES SOUND LIKE?
Squeaks, squeals, squawks, hums, whistles, whines, rich
    musical tones
not like human beings
language of clicks

HOW DO SCIENTISTS KNOW IF MESSAGES GET THROUGH?
Take turns in "speaking"

If information can be written under the questions or new questions can be formulated, fewer words need to be written down, because much thinking has already gone into the question. The context is already provided.

The danger of formulating questions in advance, however, is that the child will read only with a view to answering a few questions and not to gain a broad understanding of the subject. It is more a matter of learning style. Heavy demands are placed on the teacher who works with children during the formal report process. One of the teacher's most important roles is to observe the individual child's learning process. Nowhere will it be more visible than in the taking of notes and in the use of those notes. Children must have a deep understanding of their information to take notes effectively, which is all the more reason to use picture books and allow children adequate time to talk about their subject.

Some children will be helped by drawing: beneath the notes, a child draws a whale with wavy lines that connote sound passage. Children will have a host of approaches to using drawings to enhance visual memory features. Drawings themselves can be advance organizers for thinking; they are abstractions of ideas. They are ideographs much like the hieroglyphs of the Egyptians and the ideograms of the Chinese, which resemble the ideas themselves. The process may seem slow and painstaking, but remember that most children never learn how they learn, never acquire the skills to abstract and reconstitute the information they have gathered at one time for use at a later time. The skill of abstracting is one that is developed over a lifetime of learning, but it can begin as early as the primary years.

ACTION: DISCUSS THE NOTES WITHOUT USING THE BOOK.

Children should tell their partners, or a small group of three to four children, about their subjects but without using their books or their other sources of information. If some notes cannot be used, children may wish to go back to the book to see if they can expand the note or if the problem was in understanding the concept.

ACTION: WRITE A TEXT FROM MEMORY.

At this point, the children write for ten minutes without using books or notes. They try to write a letter or a short piece about what they have learned that day and exchange their letter with another child or with the teacher. It is most important that the letters go out to others; otherwise they may resemble more abbreviated texts, such as the notes. The letters can be answered orally or in writing. The above process is a good one to use on a daily basis. The child gets used to integrating the information into the previous data through oral and written discourse. The process of writing is too easily delayed; the ten-minute writing time helps young writers learn to listen to their own thoughts about the matter.

Children can experiment with other points of view about their data. Although in some cases this is pure speculation, it is good practice for understanding the nuances in information. For example, points of speculation about whale communication could include these: Is the turn-taking really conversation? Maybe the whales only produce feelings with the messages rather than transmitting specific information. The ten-minute writing session may involve just the statement of other possible viewpoints about the data. You might ask, "If someone came up with an opposite point of view about what you have found so far, how would that point of view be expressed?"

FIRST IN A SERIES   It is very difficult to help children understand how to put reading and writing to work if they write only one report. First attempts are not usually very strong, because the child is learning the process. In a group of eight children, however, there will probably be one or two who demonstrate a good understanding of the process. Their products will be strong, and the other children will catch a vision of how they went about their work through their oral sharing.

Children will also be learning about better sources of information and about other subjects they might prefer to the one in the first report. It is hard to choose a subject well the first time. Therefore, the second report ought to follow the first within several weeks or even go back to back with the first.

I find that the third report is usually the best for all children. Both second and third reports tend to be more lengthy as the children learn to control their information. The principle of brevity for clear writing, however, is one that remains throughout the process of reporting. Teachers do not need to push for longer reports; they become longer because the child knows how to work with the process and better understands the subject.

SUMMARY OF PRINCIPLES TO THIS POINT

Children's first venture into more formal reporting is a short one, both in time and in the length of piece they compose. Children choose their first topics on the basis of what they already know something about. Controls for both length and topic choice are geared to help children discover that the process of reporting helps them learn more about what they already know. Children should end the first phase of reporting with the notion that they *do* know a body of information, that they can gain recognition for themselves as learners.

Several recurring processes are involved in learning how to report: discussion, data gathering, abstracting, and writing. Listed in steps, the process may look like this:

1. Make a list of things you know how to do, or areas of knowledge you feel you know something about.
2. Discuss the list with another person or with a small group, listening to the voices as they work with the information.

3. Choose a topic from the list and make a web. Talk about the web.
4. Focus in on an aspect of the web or work to expand the web if it is needed. Or start a new web if the choice was not a good one.
5. Formulate questions about the part of the web you have chosen.
6. Find some reading material about your subject. Make a web from the reading material if that will help.
7. Become involved in a mini-lesson about a section of information you need. See how notes and an abstract of a text are made.
8. Make notes, either by posting them under the questions you formulated or by keeping them on the same page.
9. Talk about your subject using your notes.
10. Talk about your subject without using your notes.
11. Write a letter to someone explaining the information about your subject. Write rapidly for ten minutes.
12. Read and gather more information, take notes again, discuss them, and then write another letter about the data.

For their first report, children probably won't finish more than two or three sequences of gathering information, discussing it, and writing the rapid, ten-minute letters. This is enough data gathering to get the feel of the process. Students can then move on to organize their information.

ORGANIZING INFORMATION There are many ways to organize information. A few principles may help. (I will try to demonstrate using the material about whales and their communication.)

1. Read through the notes with a second piece of scrap paper. Whenever the subject changes, put down a title for the new subject. After the titles have been written,

decide the best order to help the reader understand the subject.

2. Write a piece of fiction. If the information can be embedded in a story, with the facts used to control the story, then there is a natural order to the data in the unfolding narrative. I could write a story about how a whale communicated with another whale a long distance away and how that communication was used within the complex of a drama.

3. Include the information in a poem in which you try to express whale sounds, along with how whales communicate.

4. Look back at the questions and determine the best order for presenting them, deciding how the answer to one question leads to the next question, etc.

5. Try to understand where the current focus, whale communication, fits in with the broader subject of whales themselves. Answer this question and make it a governing principle in the presentation: *Why should people understand the importance of whales' communication with one another?*

PRINCIPLES FOR KEEPING THE INVESTIGATION ALIVE Whether the report is the child's first or third, or is short or long, for many it is not easy to maintain an interest over time. There is a certain amount of tedium that may go along with any investigation. Nevertheless, there are some tips you can give to children to help them from the outset of their study process. These are listed here with brief discussions:

1. *Plan for discussion with discovery.* Discussion, with specifics on discovery, helps keep voice alive. Voice, the sense of authority and control of information, is what maintains a child's interest.

2. *Review.* Help children to realize what they have accomplished thus far by asking them to relate the steps they have

carried out to this point. This also serves to set them up for the next report.

3. *Tone.* Make a tape recording of your work with the children. Listen for these things:

   a. Sense of wonder. A sense of awe and wonder at the structure and detail in the universe is most important. Wonder is a mixture of an awareness of beauty and a sense of humor at the structure and detail of the universe, as well as the ways in which people perceive the universe. There is wonder in my information and children's information, and in the *way* in which we see it.

   b. Taking stock of the situation. This is where we have been and where we are now. There is where *you* have been and are now. Where there is confusion, or I sense it, I review for the group or individual. The basic tone is: *of course we know where we are.*

   c. What's next. I listen to see if I explain for myself and for the children what is next. I say where I've been and what my plans are.

4. *Audience.* Is there an audience beyond the teacher who needs the information? What will happen to these products? Will the children have a specific audience who will share their reports—a close friend, the entire class, a teacher, a parent, etc.?

5. *Learning so far.* Have children share what they have learned—a key fact, and something that made them wonder.

6. *Write to the children.* For children who struggle, write notes to them telling them what you've noticed about what they've expressed or what you know they know about their subject (or tell them orally). Write notes to children to help them see what problems they've solved; no matter how small the problem, let them know. For children who struggle, it is hard work to find these data.

7. *Your own demonstrations.* It is essential that you, the teacher, do your own report so that children may witness and learn from your learning process. Reports, like writing and reading, depend on children's witnessing your involvement in the process, which is essential for the right tone.

8. *Broader questions for teachers to ask themselves.* These questions relate to room conditions and practices that affect successful reporting by children:

   a. Room responsibilities. How well do students accept broad room responsibilities? How self-sufficient are they?

   b. Reading/writing process. Students should be well versed in working daily with books and writing. Both the reading and the writing process should be familiar to them.

   c. Time. Writing reports is a daily activity requiring a good block of time. If you consider the importance of being able to use all the language processes in putting literacy to work, the time children take for their reports will come into proper focus. An entire language block is a good use of time (sixty to ninety minutes minimum).

   d. Grouping practices. If children have been grouped homogeneously, then a sense of community and responsibility are affected. Some children are "in" and others "out," thus affecting children's sense of self-sufficiency and their ability to function independently.

BRINGING THE SHORT REPORT TO COMPLETION—SOME CAUTIONS
Children have now worked on organizing and should be near final copy. Although this chapter has presented one approach to writing reports, showing steps that are useful to most writers, some children may not need some of the steps, a few may complete their work in a few days, whereas others may need several weeks. These steps exist to help you understand what

components may be useful to most students. Generally, the principles of talking, gathering data, and writing create a productive approach to thinking for most learners. But more steps are provided here for you to help children than may be necessary for all children. The steps are to be used *after* you have observed the progress and the needs of your own students. The conditions for effective reporting listed above are more important than the methods described in this chapter.

Completing the short report is not much different from completing any piece of writing. Reading the report aloud to other children to listen for continuity of information is helpful. Writing partners or other children can estimate places where conventions may be needed by circling words that may be misspelled and marking places where commas or periods may be needed.

An outline can be a useful tool to help children understand the organization of their pieces. Take your own piece, place it on one side of the overhead projector and compose an outline on the other side of the acetate.

The best use of an outline is to show how a piece has been put together. Using an outline before writing tends to control material and prevents the learner from listening to the data. When I was a student in school we were usually required to attach an outline to our papers. I found that the only way I could make a good outline was to compose one *after* I'd written the composition, that a good outline demonstrated that each subpoint followed every major heading and idea. Once the writer has established a voice, and the writing flows as the writer anticipates the reader's need for information, an outline can be useful in showing how the information has been ordered. It is also a help in showing what needs to be deleted.

WHAT NEXT WITH THE REPORT?

The purpose of the report is to help children enjoy the process of discovering information on the way to learning some of the tools that will help them sustain more complex reports. If some children decide that learning the process was enough, and that the topic they pursued was not of sufficient interest to keep going, they can choose a new one for the next round. How soon the student begins to work again needs to be carefully considered. Some may need a week's delay, others longer; most need to start immediately if the first reporting process has been one of effective discovery. Others may find that the first report is an excellent launch pad for a longer, more sustained effort. They know more about their subject, have discovered new material they have not yet read, and can think of new ways of reporting their subject through different genres.

INVOLVE
THE LIBRARY AND
THE LIBRARIAN

When reports are working well, the librarian is usually at the center, helping children develop their topics. Some schools don't have librarians; some schools have few books, and the teacher has to help children learn to use the town library. In other instances, the very reports children write can be used as valuable resources for other children in the class and in the school.

In the best school libraries, some books are in short supply because of high student interest. Books on whales, sharks, prehistoric animals, horses, dogs and cats, outer space, automobiles, and sports are hard to keep in the library. Children can be recruited to write and supply good information books for the library. Standards must be kept high for such books. For example, a child who wrote a strong first one-and-a-half-page report could be asked to develop the report into a small book for circulation in the class or school library. It not only contributes to those resource collections, but it also adds a vital sense of audience to the child's own writing. Illustrations will be an important part of the report and may mean that a child can collaborate with another child to illustrate and help complete the project.

INTERVIEWING

Interviewing is an excellent approach to use with reports. When children interview a person who is both knowledgeable and enthusiastic about a subject, they often take on the expert's voice and try the voice in their own writing. Interviews take preparation but contribute much to children's understanding of what it means to know a subject well. There are often timely moments in the course of preparing a report when interviews give a lift to a lagging project.

SECOND AND THIRD REPORTS
The process is essentially the same for the second and third report as for the first. If the child already has a strong voice, then oral sharing may not be needed. Still, children's sharing of what they have learned and how they went about learning it will be helpful to others in the class. Sharing at the end of work time will continue. Regular writing and the exchange of letters will also be important to help learners get started. Again, there are exceptions. Some children know what they wish to do and do not need outside interruption. Extra steps or the overuse of process merely holds them back. Teacher observation will be important here. You know what to observe because you have also been involved in the process of composing reports.

FINAL REFLECTIONS
Learning to write a report takes time. During our school careers, most of us began to write reports in the fifth or sixth grade and sometimes much later. When we did, we suddenly "jumped from the bridge" producing a required ten- to twelve-page report with three references. We didn't choose the subject and we had no notion of how to use our time. Seldom were we actually shown how to choose a subject or take notes by a teacher who actually did the report with us.

The object of the whole report process is to help students find a territory of information they know something about, and then enjoy the process of learning still more by listening to their reading and to the texts they compose. The report should become a natural part of children's lives and a tool for important learning. With the best of help, using all the procedures recommended in this chapter, it will probably take at least three reports before most children feel comfortable with this type of nonfiction.

In the first set of reports, if two children in a class of twenty achieve a sense of control of their subjects I consider that a normal pattern of performance. Those two children, however, if given enough opportunity to discuss their process and their vision of what it means to share their information and their discoveries, will have an important effect on the second set of reports. Possibly another eight to ten children will join them in understanding the process. Depending on how it is spaced and paced for the remaining children, the third set of reports will pick up a few more, although there will still be children for whom report writing remains foreign and difficult. Informal reporting, as outlined in Chapter 2, may still be the best approach for them. Remember, most people go a lifetime and rarely find out that writing nonfiction reports can become a part of their lives. Yet those people who can acquire this tool early will never lose either the joy in learning or the power to learn.

MORE ADVANCED REPORTING

Choosing a report topic is not the exclusive diet of young learners. Once children have acquired a rich sense of process they ought to move into all kinds of reports, in all areas of the curriculum. Furthermore, children ought to live with a curricular philosophy that allows them time to pursue areas of interest on their own.

references

Atwell, Nancie. 1987. *In the Middle: Writing, Reading, and Learning with Adolescents*. Portsmouth, NH: Boynton/Cook.

Flower, Linda S., and J. R. Hayes. 1981. "Plans That Guide the Composing Process." In *Writing: The Nature, Development, and Teaching of Written Communication*, ed. by C. H. Frederiksen and J. F. Dominic. Vol. 2, pp. 39–58. Hillsdale, NJ: Erlbaum.

Grosvenor, Donna K., and Larry K. Foster. 1977. *The Blue Whale*. Washington, DC: National Geographic Society for Young Explorers.

Heath, Shirley Brice. 1987. "The Literate Essay: Myths and Ethnography." In *Language, Literacy, and Culture*. Norwood, NJ: Ablex.

Sowers, Susan. 1985. "The Story and the 'All About' Book." In *Breaking Ground: Teachers Relate Reading and Writing in the Elementary School*, ed. by Jane Hansen, Thomas Newkirk, and Donald Graves. Portsmouth, NH: Heinemann.

Watson, Jane Werner. 1975. *Whales—Friendly Dolphins and Mighty Giants of the Sea*. Illustrated by Richard Amundsen. New York: Golden Press.

Wigginton, Eliot, ed. Various dates. Foxfire Series. New York: Doubleday.

Woodhouse, Kate, ed. 1974. *The Life of Sea Mammals*. A Macdonald Education Book. London: Macdonald.

index

Please remember that this is a library book,
and that it belongs only temporarily to each
person who uses it. Be considerate. Do
not write in this, or any, library book.

DATE DUE

2·15·02			
JE 16 '02			
GAYLORD			PRINTED IN U.S.A.